f Interest

Los intereses creados

A Dual-Language Book

Jacinto Benavente

Edited and Translated by
STANLEY APPELBAUM

DOVER PUBLICATIONS, INC.
Mineola, New York

Theatrical Rights

This Dover edition may be used in its entirety, in adaptation, or in any other way for professional or amateur theatrical productions in the United States without fee, permission, or acknowledgment.

Bibliographical Note

This Dover edition, first published in 2004, includes the full Spanish text of *Los intereses creados,* first published in Madrid in 1908 (see the Introduction for further bibliographical details), accompanied by a new English translation by Stanley Appelbaum, who also wrote the Introduction, Appendix, and footnotes.

International Standard Book Number: 0-486-43086-3

Manufactured in the United States of America
Dover Publications, Inc., 31 East 2nd Street, Mineola, N.Y. 11501

Contents

INTRODUCTION

Benavente's Life and Works

Born in Madrid in 1866, Jacinto Benavente y Martínez grew up as a *señorito:* the scion of a wealthy, prominent family (his father was a leading pediatrician), well educated and a member of good society. After elementary and secondary schooling at prestigious institutions, he entered the Universidad Central of Madrid in 1882, studying law (these studies are clearly reflected in the scenes with the Doctor in *Los intereses creados*). But after his father died in 1885, he left the university and devoted himself to his overriding passion for show business (as a child he had owned a toy theater and had been a frequent playgoer). He became an actor, and for a while he toured Europe as director of a circus (one major encyclopedia states that he had fallen in love with one of the equestriennes).

In 1892 he published a volume called *Teatro fantástico* (Plays of the Imagination), containing eight short closet dramas. Around the same time he also tried his hand at poems and short stories. The first play of his to be performed, *El nido ajeno* (Another's Nest;[1] 1894), about a man in love with his brother's wife, was too unpleasant for the rather frivolous Spanish audiences of the day, but Benavente achieved a breakthrough success two years later with a milder social satire, *Gente conocida* (Well-Known People). His first internationally acclaimed play was *La noche del sábado* (Witches' Sabbath; 1903), about the shady side of cosmopolitan society. From then on, he continued to be the most popular purveyor of sophisticated, but fundamentally conservative theater pieces to the playgoers of Spain, and his biography is chiefly the listing of his numerous rapidly, but carefully and cunningly written stage works. In 1909 he founded a children's theater and wrote worthwhile pieces for it.

1. English-language reference books give a wide variety of renderings of the Spanish titles of Benavente's plays (indicating that most of his plays have not become familiar fare in British and American theaters). For simplicity, this Introduction uses only one, arbitrarily chosen rendering for each.

Down through the First World War (during which he alienated some of his contemporaries by his marked sympathies for the German side) Benavente was a major glory of what has been called the Silver Age (Edad de Plata) of Spanish literature, music, and art. He was friendly with the Modernistas (the spiritual heirs of the nineteenth-century French Parnassians and Symbolists)[2] and with the members of the so-called Generation of 1898, though he didn't share their loftier aims,[3] and the 98-ers must have been irritated with his blatantly greater success in the theater. From the viewpoint of Spanish theatrical history, Benavente's quiet sophistication was a direct challenge to the ranting magniloquence of José Echegaray (1832–1916).[4] Moreover, Benavente's prolific output, with its almost bewildering variety of subject and tone, was unique.

During this same first creative period, Benavente, who never married (he lived with his mother until her death) was a notorious playboy. In addition, he edited magazines (beginning in 1899), wrote a popular newspaper column (from 1906 to 1908 and 1914 to 1916), and flirted with politics.

After a savaging by certain critics, who called his plays facile, rhetorical, superficial, devoid of stage action (which was replaced by narratives), and lacking in true character studies, Benavente produced no new plays from 1920 to 1924, but he remained active in the theater. In 1920 he became director of the Teatro Español. He directed plays and sometimes acted in them. He was on a tour of South America and the United States when he learned in 1922 that he had won that year's Nobel Prize for literature. In the same year he founded a movie studio, the Société des Films Benavente, which produced two pictures.

The scores of plays he wrote after resuming his efforts in 1924 are not as highly regarded as his earlier ones, but he continued to be a national figure, the recipient of awards and honors (he had been an in-

---

2. The brightest light of *modernismo* was the Nicaraguan-born poet and story writer Rubén Darío (1867–1916). In *Los intereses creados,* the leitmotiv of sky-versus-ground (Leander's daydreaming and Crispin's grim practicality) is almost surely an echo of the same theme, which recurs in a number of Darío's prose and verse pieces. 3. Benavente was never as serious as, for instance, Miguel de Unamuno (1864–1936), nor as experimental as Ramón del Valle-Inclán (1866–1936). 4. Echagaray (who, coincidentally, was a client of Benavente's father) had revitalized the slumping Spanish post-Romantic theater in 1881 with his masterpiece, *El gran Galeoto* (The Great Go-Between). When Echegaray was chosen to share the 1905 Nobel Prize for literature (with the Provençal poet Frédéric Mistral, 1830–1914), Benavente did not participate in the protests against that choice raised by many littérateurs.

active member of the Royal Academy since 1912). During the Civil War of 1936–1939, he lived in relative seclusion in Valencia. After Franco's victory he was back in the limelight, comfortable under the fascist régime. In 1945 he once more directed a troupe in Argentina. He continued to turn out plays until his death in Madrid in 1954 (three new ones were produced that year). Having written up to five plays in some years, he had amassed a grand total of some 172 (tallies vary).

His oeuvre includes both realistic and more imaginative plays: regional and folk plays (*costumbrista*); satires; symbolic, psychological, patriotic, and historical works; even skits and librettos for musicals (*zarzuelas*). His plays take place in a variety of milieus: Madrid middle-class, cosmopolitan, provincial-town, rural, and fantasy. His reputation as a pillar of the early twentieth-century Spanish theater is secure, and his plays are still performed in Spain, but at the present day he is not an international force, and some encyclopedia articles about him are openly disrespectful. His most famous disciple was Gregorio Martínez Sierra (1881–1947), whose most famous play was *Canción de cuna* (Cradle Song).

Besides *Los intereses creados*, which is the subject of the following section of this Introduction, and *La malquerida*,[5] at least eight Benavente plays have been performed in New York.

Los intereses creados (*The Bonds of Interest*)

Benavente's fifty-third play, *Los intereses creados* was first published in Madrid in 1908 by Velasco, Imp., as Volume 23 in the series "Teatro español." It was dedicated to Rafael Gasset, and bore the subtitle "comedia de Polichinelas, en dos actos, tres cuadros y un prólogo" (Punchinello comedy in two acts, three tableaux, and a prologue).

The play had premiered on December 9, 1907, at the Teatro Lara in Madrid. This "candy box" of a theater, named for Cándido Lara, who founded it in 1880, had originally offered only light

5. Produced in 1913, *La malquerida* (The Ill-Loved Woman; best known in England and the United States as "The Passion Flower") contains Benavente's major serious feminine role, that of a woman in love with her stepfather. The role was created by María Guerrero (Spain's answer to Bernhardt and Duse), and was played in New York in 1920 by the eminent tragedienne Nance O'Neil, who had a very respectable local run and then toured extensively with the play.

entertainments, but by 1907 was staging more demanding plays and was known for the excellent actors attached to it.

It has been said that Benavente wrote the play in pique at a moment when he was hounded by creditors. Some literary historians have seen as his direct source the little-known play by Lope de Vega (1562–1635) *El caballero de Illescas,* in which a penniless man arrives in a strange town and angles for a rich heiress. As will be suggested below, a much wider range of sources could have been at Benavente's disposal.

Los intereses creados was instantly acclaimed in Europe, and most connoisseurs still consider it the author's best work (with other votes for *La malquerida* and a scattering of other plays); it has been called the most representative of his genius and art, though it is atypical in its unspecified setting, unreal milieu, and use of commedia dell'arte figures. Its placing of the action in the seventeenth century allows for sumptuous costuming (when the author's wishes are respected); the period is echoed in the text of the play by references to galley slaves and by the men's wearing of swords, among other things. The "imaginary country" where the action occurs is surely Italy, from much internal evidence.

The single most striking feature of *Los intereses creados* is its revival of certain elements of the commedia dell'arte, as announced in the Prologue.[6] This "professional acting" (arte = guild), as opposed to performances by scholarly Renaissance amateurs, arose in Italy early in the sixteenth century and remained popular throughout Europe, thanks to Italian touring troupes and their emulators, well into the eighteenth, with some repercussions felt to the present day. (The work of Molière, Marivaux, and Beaumarchais owes it an enormous debt.) Its sources included ancient Roman comedy (the source of the boastful soldier, for instance), medieval jongleurs, and fairground performances. Generally the actors improvised the dialogue on the basis of elaborate scenarios (with plots often vastly more complicated than Benavente's). Commedia dell'arte (also called Italian comedy) was known for its array of typical roles (actors would become associated

6. Benavente's Prologue is like a contrary counterpart to the Prologue of the 1892 opera *I pagliacci* (libretto and music by Leoncavallo), in which the clown Tonio announces that the comic proceedings are *not* to be laughed at, because a slice of real life will be presented. (In this footnote and the three following, the Dover translator is not claiming that Benavente was familiar with the literary antecedents mentioned, but is merely pointing out that he might have been [Benavente knew English, French, and Italian, and was alert to current literary trends], or at least that such ideas were in the air.)

with a single role-type), which would retain their standard characteristics no matter what specific actions they were called upon to perform in any given play. The pieces were usually comic, including a lot of slapstick (faintly echoed in Benavente's piece by the beating of the Innkeeper); the humor was frequently erotic and scatological. (Commedia dell'arte reached Spain in the first half of the sixteenth century, and became firmly established after 1574, influencing Golden Age [Siglo de Oro] drama.)

The characters in *Los intereses creados* that are most directly based on Italian-comedy figures (and bearing their traditional names) are the Doctor, the Captain, Harlequin, Columbine, Pantaloon, and Punchinello. The Doctor is the one handled most traditionally; in commedia dell'arte, *il Dottore* was a pedantic physician or lawyer.[7] The Captain (in Italian, *il Capitano*) is also the traditional boastful, but not really brave soldier; oddly, Benavente disturbed the tone of the role (and of the whole play) by giving his Captain one heartfelt, bitter tirade against war profiteers who deserve to have the populace rise up against them. Harlequin (*Arlecchino* in Italian) was originally the second comic servant (*zanni*) in commedia dell'arte, a fool who got into many scrapes; in Benavente, there's little left of this; his Harlequin is cast in a different mold, that of the parasitic poetaster, which has a separate dramatic genealogy. Benavente's Columbine is also much feebler than the original scheming servant wench *Colombina;* she's still in love with Harlequin, but never interacts with him in the course of the play, and never initiates a stratagem; she merely behaves pertly and delivers a couple of distinctly infra-Wildean epigrams. Pantaloon (*Pantalone* in Italian) was traditionally the twitted father of the ingénue, opposed to her romance with the young lover; the only usual characteristic remaining in Benavente is that he's a rich merchant—but with a negligible part as a noisy creditor. Punchinello (in Italian, *Pulcinella*) became such an overridingly popular figure by the eighteenth century that he is said to have caused the decline of commedia dell'arte as a viable team effort; in Benavente he is still amoral and antisocial, and the traditional hump on his back is mentioned.

All in all, what did Benavente gain by using these largely watered-down figures instead of ordinary characters with everyday names? It has been said that he adopted the old role-names to avoid alienating

7. The passage in which Benavente's Doctor absolves Leander by manipulating commas is uncannily similar to the very end of Gilbert and Sullivan's *Iolanthe* (1882), in which the Lord Chancellor radically alters fairy law by inserting one word into a vital regulation.

his audience with the unpleasant truths he was proclaiming, truths that would be made more palatable by this "distancing" (like Brecht's *Verfremdung*).

Among the other characters, Sylvia (*Silvia* is one of the many names used for that role-type in commedia dell'arte) is lovable for her loyalty. Leander is decidedly not a typical bland Italian-comedy young lover; his real roots lie in other traditions;[8] curiously, at the play's premiere the part was played by a woman (because of Leander's weak, passive nature, it is said), and this continued to be a tradition in Spain for some time. Madam Sirena is a descendant of such native Spanish panders and procuresses as Trotaconventos in *El libro de buen amor* by Juan Ruiz, Arcipreste de Hita (ca. 1340) and Celestina in the *Tragicomedia de Calisto y Melibea* by Fernando de Rojas (1499).

Of course, the main role in Benavente's play—a spectacular, kaleidoscopic starring part—is that of Crispin, who pulls all the strings. This role, that of a clever, devil-may-care servant (in this particular play, a pretended servant) who promotes his master's love affair, goes back to that of the *gracioso* (comic) in Golden Age drama; but the *gracioso,* in turn, was descended from the role-type of Brighella in commedia dell'arte, the first comic servant (*zanni*), the clever one who controlled situations.[9]

Los intereses creados had a triumphant career in Spain. Benavente himself occasionally recited the Prologue at performances, or played the entire role of Crispin. In 1916 he wrote a (far inferior) sequel, *La ciudad alegre y confiada* (The Happy, Confiding City), in which some of the old characters return and Crispin achieves the political power he had had in mind for himself in the 1907 play. In 1915 Benavente had been presented with an illuminated manuscript of *Los intereses creados,* hand-lettered and sumptuously illustrated by Gabriel Ochoa, in the name of all the actors in

---

8. Leander is very much like the vagabond hero of Gogol's *Inspector General* (1836), whom the townspeople entertain lavishly in the belief he's a great dignitary. From a different point of view, he resembles the Romantic-era flawed hero who is redeemed by the true love of a good woman; the archetypical example, perhaps, is Wagner's Flying Dutchman (1843), but only two years before Benavente's play the theme had been revitalized in David Belasco's *The Girl of the Golden West.* 9. Crispin has also been compared to Puss-in-Boots (in the 1697 Perrault tale, itself based on one by Straparola, ca. 1550), who ruthlessly elevates his feckless master from rags ro riches. Crispin's speech about separating the good and bad in man into two entirely distinct persons is also reminiscent of Stevenson's "Strange Case of Dr. Jekyll and Mr. Hyde" (1886).

Spain. In 1918 he directed a film version of the 1907 play. *Los intereses creados* has been regularly revived in Spain, and was produced in Madrid as least as late as 1992.

In New York the play hasn't fared so well. In 1919 it was the very first work staged by the Theatre Guild—with the poet Edna St. Vincent Millay playing Columbine—but it was neither a critical nor a financial success. It did no better ten years later when the distinguished actor Walter Hampden produced it at his own theater, starring as Crispin. The subsequent performances were off-Broadway: in the round at the Circle in the Square, with an adapted text, in 1951 (the critics' reactions to the play itself were highly mixed); in 1958 at the Sheridan Square Playhouse; and in a heavily adapted musical version called *Crisp*, 1981.

The English translation, performed as written, or used as the basis of the stage adaptations, was by John Garrett Underhill. First published in the journal *The Drama* in 1915,[10] and included in 1917 in the first of Underhill's four volumes of *Plays by Jacinto Benavente*, it was later anthologized several times in whole or in part. The catchy English rendering of the title, "The Bonds of Interest," is Underhill's. (The Spanish, baldly translated, would yield "The Created Interests." Perhaps the ideal rendering is "Vested Interests.") Underhill's version is basically correct and often flavorful (though a bit stiff for modern tastes), but is marred by a fair number of careless errors (e.g., the absurd "Emperor of Mantua" instead of "ambassador from Mantua," and such mistakings of verb endings and pronouns as "he insisted on being faithful to me" as a rendering of *supe serle fiel*), by a lack of recognition of idioms ("over four princesses" for *más de cuatro princesas*), by words not fully translated from Spanish ("protocols of the process" instead of "dossier of the criminal investigation"), and by a constant tendency to expand the text with his own verbiage, often needlessly and sometimes with unfortunate results.[11]

10. No. 20, the November 1915 issue (a quarterly published in Chicago by the Drama League of America). 11. As when he adds, after "She has reconciled herself to your death," "She hopes for nothing else"(!!!). In Act One, when Leander is being deliberately taciturn, Underhill will have him speak seven words when the Spanish has one. (Other features of Underhill's translation are mentioned in the next section of the Introduction.)

The Nature of This Edition

The Spanish text provided is as authentic and correct as possible. The new English translation follows that text faithfully, neither omitting nor adding any concept, though it attempts to be modern, flavorful, and idiomatic, and (because new Dover translations of plays are meant to be performed—see the statement on the copyright page) it is intentionally conversational, sometimes using an additional English word or two to make the speech sound more natural.

Unlike Underhill, this translation, retains the original Spanish two-act form (he called the *Cuadro segundo* of the first act "Act Two," and made the second act "Act Three"). It also, unlike Underhill, retains the division of the *cuadros* into *escenas*. These *escenas* (a practice in play-text publication extending into the early twentieth century from at least the seventeenth) do not indicate a change of locale, a blackout, or any other discontinuity in the action; they merely indicate the entrance or exit of a major character, and the stage directions that immediately follow the heading "Escena" list the characters now on stage. The Dover translator, hard put to find any word but "scene" to render *escena,* was thus constrained to render *cuadro* as "tableau," though the *cuadros* are precisely what we would call "scenes" nowadays (changes of locale, breaks in the action).

In order to make this a true performing version, the poem at the end of Act One has been translated into English verse (with even more rhymes than the original Spanish, which often assonates; it proved impossible, however, to reflect the several shorter verses in the Spanish), and the dossier clauses altered by inserting or deleting a comma (near the end of Act Two) have been somewhat adapted to permit of analogous word play in English. In both cases, strictly literal translations have been provided in an Appendix.[12]

A final word, on the stage directions. Underhill wisely omitted some of the technical stagecraft terms that are found in many of them in Spanish, but such an omission couldn't be countenanced in a complete, facing-page translation like this one. Benavente's stage had flats (cloth attached to framework) at the sides (in the "wings"), wholly or partially out of the view of the audience. These flats (*bastidores* in Spanish), which ran parallel to the proscenium arch, had corridor-like

12. Underhill's verse translation of the poem has choppy meter, and departs farther and farther from the original meaning as it goes along. His version of the dossier clauses is nearly incomprehensible.

spaces between them (*cajas* in Spanish), which were numbered, the first being the one closest to the proscenium. Thus, when the Spanish stage directions instruct an actor to enter from, or into, the *primera* or *segunda,* the word *caja* is understood, and the translation uses the wording "first [second] wing-space." Naturally, these directions are totally irrelevant to a modern production.[13]

13. Some stage directions in Act Two read: *segunda derecha, o sea el pasillo.* The translator has been unable to find a definition for *pasillo* ("corridor, passageway") as a structural offstage element (it has other theatrical meanings which cannot possibly apply here). The *o sea* ("or") may possibly mean that *pasillo* is the equivalent of *segunda derecha* (but then, why would it be used only in a few instances?), or (less likely grammatically) that it is some separate passageway in the wings, or else (the solution favored by this translator, but without proofs) that the *pasillo* is an imaginary offstage corridor in Leander's house leading into the onstage room.

The Bonds of Interest

Los intereses creados

Personajes

DOÑA SIRENA
SILVIA
LA SEÑORA DE POLICHINELA
COLOMBINA
LAURA
RISELA
LEANDRO
CRISPÍN
EL DOCTOR
POLICHINELA
ARLEQUÍN
EL CAPITÁN
PANTALÓN
EL HOSTELERO
EL SECRETARIO
MOZO 1.º DE LA HOSTERÍA
MOZO 2.º
ALGUACILILLO 1.º
ALGUACILILLO 2.º

La acción pasa en un pais imaginario, a principios del siglo XVII.

Characters

MADAM SIRENA
SYLVIA
PUNCHINELLO'S WIFE
COLUMBINE
LAURA
RISELA
LEANDER
CRISPIN
THE DOCTOR [OF LAW]
PUNCHINELLO
HARLEQUIN
THE CAPTAIN
PANTALOON
THE INNKEEPER
THE [DOCTOR'S] SECRETARY
1ST INN SERVANT
2ND INN SERVANT
1ST CONSTABLE
2ND CONSTABLE

The play takes place in an imaginary country at the beginning of the seventeenth century.

Acto primero

Prólogo

Telón corto en primer término, con puerta al foro, y en ésta un tapiz.
Recitado por el personaje CRISPÍN

He aquí el tinglado de la antigua farsa, la que alivió en posadas aldeanas el cansancio de los trajinantes, la que embobó en las plazas de humildes lugares a los simples villanos, la que juntó en ciudades populosas a los más variados concursos, como en París sobre el Puente Nuevo, cuando Tabarín desde su tablado de feria solicitaba la atención de todo transeúnte, desde el espetado doctor que detiene un momento su docta cabalgadura para desarrugar por un instante la frente, siempre cargada de graves pensamientos, al escuchar algún donaire de la alegre farsa, hasta el pícaro hampón, que allí divierte sus ocios horas y horas, engañando al hambre con la risa; y el prelado y la dama de calidad, y el gran señor desde sus carrozas, como la moza alegre y el soldado, y el mercader y el estudiante. Gente de toda condición, que en ningún otro lugar se hubiera reunido, comunicábase allí su regocijo, que muchas veces, más que de la farsa, reía el grave de ver reír al risueño, y el sabio al bobo, y los pobretes de ver reír a los grandes señores, ceñudos de ordinario, y los grandes de ver reír a los pobretes, tranquilizada su conciencia con pensar: ¡también los pobres ríen! Que nada prende tan pronto de unas almas en otras como esta simpatía de la risa. Alguna vez, también subió la farsa a palacios de príncipes, altísimos señores, por humorada de sus dueños, y no fué allí menos libre

Act One

Prologue

Act curtain far downstage, with an entrance to the rear of the stage; a cloth is draped over that entrance. The Prologue is spoken by the character CRISPIN:

Here before you is the simple platform on which was performed the farce of yesteryear, that farce which, in village inns, alleviated the weariness of the long-distance haulers; which, in the squares of humble towns, fascinated the unassuming rustics; which, in populous cities, assembled the most varied gatherings—for instance, on the Pont-Neuf in Paris, when from his fairground booth Tabarin[1] claimed the attention of every passerby, from the solemn doctor who momentarily reined in his well-trained mount in order to unfurrow for an instant his brow, always laden with grave thoughts, by listening to some witticism of the merry farce, down to the rowdy criminal who spent his leisure time there hour after hour, deluding his hunger with laughter; and the prelate and the lady of quality and the great lord, seated in their carriages, as well as the jolly servant girl, the soldier, the merchant, and the student. There people of all ranks, who wouldn't have forgathered anywhere else, infected one another with their enjoyment, for often the solemn man would laugh not so much at the farce as at the sight of the easily tickled man laughing, and the sage would laugh at the ninny, the poor would laugh seeing the great lords, usually all scowls, laugh, and the grandees would laugh at the laughter of the poor, their consciences pacified by the thought: "Poor people

1. Tabarin (Antoine Girard, ca. 1584–1626) staged outdoor medicine shows on or near the Pont-Neuf ca. 1618.

y despreocupada. Fué de todos y para todos. Del pueblo recogió burlas y malicias y dichos sentenciosos, de esa filosofía del pueblo, que siempre sufre, dulcificada por aquella resignación de los humildes de entonces, que no lo esperaban todo de este mundo, y por eso sabían reírse del mundo sin odio y sin amargura. Ilustró después su plebeyo origen con noble ejecutoria: Lope de Rueda, Shakespeare, Molière, como enamorados príncipes de cuento de hadas, elevaron a Cenicienta al más alto trono de la Poesía y el Arte. No presume de tan gloriosa estirpe esta farsa, que por curiosidad de su espíritu inquieto os presenta un poeta de ahora. Es una farsa *guiñolesca,* de asunto disparatado, sin realidad alguna. Pronto veréis cómo cuanto en ella sucede no pudo suceder nunca, que sus personajes no son ni semejan hombres y mujeres, sino muñecos o fantoches de cartón y trapo, con groseros hilos, visibles a poca luz y al más corto de vista. Son las mismas grotescas máscaras de aquella comedia de Arte italiano, no tan regocijadas como solían, porque han meditado mucho en tanto tiempo. Bien conoce el autor que tan primitivo espectáculo no es el más digno de un culto auditorio de estos tiempos; así, de vuestra cultura tanto como de vuestra bondad se ampara. El autor sólo pide que aniñéis cuanto sea posible vuestro espíritu. El mundo está ya viejo y chochea; el Arte no se resigna a envejecer, y por parecer niño finge balbuceos . . . Y he aquí cómo estos viejos polichinelas pretenden hoy divertiros con sus niñerías.

Mutación

laugh, too!" For nothing is so quickly contagious between souls as this sympathetic laughter. At times the farce also ascended to the palaces of princes, most exalted lords, through some caprice of the masters, and there it was no less liberated and carefree. It belonged to everyone and addressed everyone. From the masses it gathered practical jokes, cunning turns, and sententious sayings, that philosophy of the always suffering common man, which was sweetened by the resignation which the humble felt in those days, not expecting all things from this world, and thus able to laugh at the world without hatred or bitterness. Later on, the farce made its plebeian origin illustrious with lofty patents of nobility: Lope de Rueda,[2] Shakespeare, Molière, like the amorous princes in fairy tales, raised Cinderella to the highest throne of Poetry and Art. This farce of ours doesn't boast such a glorious lineage; a poet of today presents it to you out of the inquisitiveness of his restless mind. It's a farce for puppets; its subject is nonsensical and it's completely unreal. You will soon see that its entire action could never have taken place, that its characters aren't, and don't even resemble, men and women, but are puppets or marionettes of cardboard and rags, pulled by thick strings that are visible even in scanty light, and even to the most nearsighted. They are the same grotesque masks of that Italian commedia dell'arte, not as jolly as in the past, because in all the time that's gone by they've meditated a great deal. The author is well aware that such a primitive show is not particularly worthy of a cultured audience of this day and age; and so he claims the protection of your culture as well as your good nature. The author merely requests that you make your minds as childlike as possible. The world is already old and in its dotage, but Art refuses to grow old and, to resemble a child, it pretends to stammer. . . . And that's why these old-time Punchinellos hope to entertain you today with their childish pranks.

Change of scene.

2. Author of farces, precursor of Golden Age comedy (ca. 1510–1565).

Cuadro primero

Plaza de una ciudad. A la derecha, en primer término, fachada de una hostería con puerta practicable y en ella un aldabón. Encima de la puerta un letrero que diga: "Hostería"

Escena I

LEANDRO *y* CRISPÍN, *que salen por la segunda izquierda*

LEANDRO.—Gran ciudad ha de ser ésta, Crispín; en todo se advierte su señorío y riqueza.

CRISPÍN.—Dos ciudades hay. ¡Quiera el Cielo que en la mejor hayamos dado!

LEANDRO.—¿Dos ciudades dices, Crispín? Ya entiendo, antigua y nueva, una de cada parte del río.

CRISPÍN.—¿Qué importa el río ni la vejez ni la novedad? Digo dos ciudades como en toda ciudad del mundo: una para el que llega con dinero, y otra para el que llega como nosotros.

LEANDRO.—¡Harto es haber llegado sin tropezar con la justicia! Y bien quisiera detenerme aquí algún tiempo, que ya me cansa tanto correr tierras.

CRISPÍN.—A mí no, que es condición de los naturales, como yo, del libre reino de Picardía, no hacer asiento en parte alguna, si no es forzado y en galeras, que es duro asiento. Pero ya que sobre esta ciudad caímos y es plaza fuerte a lo que se descubre, tracemos como prudentes capitanes nuestro plan de batalla, si hemos de conquistarla con provecho.

LEANDRO.—¡Mal pertrechado ejército venimos!

CRISPÍN.—Hombres somos, y con hombres hemos de vernos.

First Tableau

A city square. Downstage right, the facade of a hostelry with a practicable door; on the door, a knocker. Over the door a sign reading "Hostelry."

Scene I

LEANDER *and* CRISPIN *enter from the second wing-space, left.*[3]

LEANDER: This must be a big city, Crispin; everything in it betokens its distinction and wealth.

CRISPIN: There are two cities. Heaven grant that we've stumbled onto the better one!

LEANDER: You say two cities, Crispin? Now I understand: the old town and the new town, one on either side of the river!

CRISPIN: Where does the river come in, or "old" and "new"? I mean: two cities, just as in every city in the world: one for the man who arrives with money, and the other for the man who arrives in our situation.

LEANDER: It's good enough to have arrived without running into the police! And I'd really like to stay here for a while, because all this dashing back and forth has tired me out.

CRISPIN: It hasn't tired *me;* it's the normal state of the natives of the free kingdom of Rascal Land,[4] of whom I'm one, never to sit themselves down anywhere, except at hard labor or as a galley rower, which is a hard place to sit on. But now that we've come upon this city, which is a fortress by all indications, let's devise our plan of battle like prudent captains, if we're to take it by storm to our advantage.

LEANDER: We make a poorly equipped army!

CRISPIN: We're men, and it's men we'll have to deal with.

---

3. On the technical terms in the stage directions, see the last section of the Introduction. 4. In the Spanish, an untranslatable pun on the Picardy region of northern France.

LEANDRO.—Por todo caudal, nuestra persona. No quisiste que nos desprendiéramos de estos vestidos, que, malvendiéndolos, hubiéramos podido juntar algún dinero.

CRISPÍN.—¡Antes me desprendiera yo de la piel que de un buen vestido! Que nada importa tanto como parecer, según va el mundo, y el vestido es lo que antes parece.

LEANDRO.—¿Qué hemos de hacer, Crispín? Que el hambre y el cansancio me tienen abatido, y mal discurro.

CRISPÍN.—Aquí no hay sino valerse del ingenio y de la desvergüenza, que sin ella nada vale el ingenio. Lo que he pensado es que tú has de hablar poco y desabrido, para darte aires de persona de calidad; de vez en cuando te permito que descargues algún golpe sobre mis costillas; a cuantos te pregunten, responde misterioso; y cuanto hables por tu cuenta, sea con gravedad; como si sentenciaras. Eres joven, de buena presencia; hasta ahora sólo supiste malgastar tus cualidades; ya es hora de aprovecharse de ellas. Ponte en mis manos, que nada conviene tanto a un hombre como llevar a su lado quien haga notar sus méritos, que en uno mismo la modestia es necedad y la propia alabanza locura, y con las dos se pierde para el mundo. Somos los hombres como mercancía, que valemos más o menos según la habilidad del mercader que nos presenta. Yo te aseguro que así fueras vidrio, a mi cargo corre que pases por diamante. Y ahora llamemos a esta hostería, que lo primero es acampar a vista de la plaza.

LEANDRO.—¿A la hostería dices? ¿Y cómo pagaremos?

CRISPÍN.—Si por tan poco te acobardas busquemos un hospital o casa de misericordia, o pidamos limosna, si a lo piadoso nos acogemos; y si a lo bravo, volvamos al camino y salteemos al primer viandante; si a la verdad de nuestros recursos nos atenemos, no son otros nuestros recursos.

LEANDRO.—Yo traigo cartas de introducción para personas de valimiento en esta ciudad, que podrán socorrernos.

CRISPÍN.—¡Rompe luego esas cartas y no pienses en tal bajeza! ¡Presentarnos a nadie como necesitados! ¡Buenas cartas de crédito son ésas! Hoy te recibirán con grandes cortesías, te dirán que su casa y su persona son tuyas, y a la segunda vez que llames a su puerta, ya te dirá el criado que su señor no está en casa ni para en ella; y a otra visita, ni te abrirán la puerta. Mundo es éste de toma y daca; lonja de contratación, casa de cambio, y antes de pedir, ha de ofrecerse.

LEANDRO.—¿Y qué podré ofrecer yo si nada tengo?

LEANDER: Our only wealth is our personal appearance. You didn't want us to part with these outfits, even though by selling them cheap we could have put a little money in our pockets.

CRISPIN: I'd sooner part with my skin than with a good suit! For there's nothing more important than looking good in this world we live in, and clothes are what catch the eye first.

LEANDER: What should we do, Crispin? For I'm so depressed with hunger and weariness that I can't invent plans.

CRISPIN: In this situation all we can do is to use our wits, and also our effrontery, because, without that, wits are no good. The plan I've come up with is for you to speak very little, and curtly when you do, to lend yourself the air of a person of quality; every so often I give you permission to beat me a little; when anyone asks you a question, make a secretive reply; anything you volunteer to say should be spoken solemnly, like a judge pronouncing sentence. You're young and attractive; up to now you've merely wasted your good points; now's the time to turn them to advantage. Put yourself in my hands, because nothing is so helpful to a man as someone alongside him pointing out his good features; when a man is on his own, modesty is folly and self-praise is madness, and when they're combined, he's lost to good society. We men are like merchandise: we're worth more or less depending on the merchant's skill in showing us off. I assure you that, even if you were glass, it's up to me to pass you off as a diamond. And now let's call at this inn, because our first requirement is to encamp within view of the theater of operations.

LEANDER: At the inn, you say? And how will we pay for it?

CRISPIN: If it takes so little to scare you, let's look for a hospice or a charity ward, or let's beg for alms, if we take the religious route; and if we take the criminal route, let's go back to the highway and rob the first man who comes by. If we face up to our true situation, we have nothing else to resort to.

LEANDER: I've got letters of recommendation to highly placed people in this city who could help us out.

CRISPIN: Tear up those letters at once and don't even think of such a low action! To introduce ourselves to anyone as being in need! Fine letters of credit those are! Today they'll receive you with great politeness and tell you their home and person are yours; the second time you call at their door, the servant will tell you his master isn't home or even in residence; and at your next visit they won't even open the door. This is a world of tit for tat, a chamber of commerce, an exchange bureau: before you request anything, you've got to offer something.

LEANDER: But what can I offer when I have nothing?

CRISPÍN.—¡En qué poco te estimas! Pues qué, un hombre por sí, ¿nada vale? Un hombre puede ser soldado, y con su valor decidir una victoria; puede ser galán o marido, y con dulce medicina curar a alguna dama de calidad o doncella de buen linaje que se sienta morir de melancolía; puede ser criado de algún señor poderoso que se aficione de él y le eleve hasta su privanza, y tantas cosas más que no he de enumerar. Para subir, cualquier escalón es bueno.

LEANDRO.—¿Y si aun ese escalón me falta?

CRISPÍN.—Yo te ofrezco mis espaldas para encumbrarte. Tú te verás en alto.

LEANDRO.—¿Y si los dos damos en tierra?

CRISPÍN.—Que ella nos sea leve. (*Llamando a la hostería con el aldabón.*) ¡Ah de la hostería! ¡Hola, digo! ¡Hostelero o demonio! ¿Nadie responde? ¿Qué casa es ésta?

LEANDRO.—¿Por qué esas voces si apenas llamasteis?

CRISPÍN.—¡Porque es ruindad hacer esperar de ese modo! (*Vuelve a llamar más fuerte.*) ¡Ah de la gente! ¡Ah de la casa! ¡Ah de todos los diablos!

HOSTELERO.—(*Dentro.*) ¿Quién va? ¿Qué voces y qué modo son éstos? No hará tanto que esperan.

CRISPÍN.—¡Ya fué mucho! Y bien nos informaron que es ésta muy ruin posada para gente noble.

Escena II

DICHOS, *el* HOSTELERO *y dos* MOZOS *que salen de la hostería*

HOSTELERO.—(*Saliendo.*) Poco a poco, que no es posada, sino hospedería, y muy grandes señores han parado en ella.

CRISPÍN.—Quisiera yo ver a esos que llamáis grandes señores. Gentecilla de poco más o menos. Bien se advierte en esos mozos, que no saben conocer a las personas de calidad, y se están ahí como pasmarotes sin atender a nuestro servicio.

HOSTELERO.—¡Por vida que sois impertinente!

LEANDRO.—Este criado mío siempre ha de extremar su celo. Buena es vuestra posada para el poco tiempo que he de parar en ella. Disponed luego un aposento para mí y otro para este criado, y ahorremos palabras.

CRISPIN: What a low idea you have of yourself! Now, I ask you, isn't a man worth anything in himself? A man can be a soldier, and his bravery can help gain a victory; he can be a suitor or a husband, and his sweet medicine can cure some lady of rank or some well-born young miss who feels she's dying of melancholy; he can be the servant of some powerful lord who takes a liking to him and raises him to the position of confidential adviser; and so many other things that I don't need to enumerate. To rise in the world, any rung of the ladder is suitable.

LEANDER: What if I lack even that rung?

CRISPIN: I'm offering you my shoulders to raise you up. You'll find yourself at the top.

LEANDER: What if we both tumble to the ground?

CRISPIN: Then, may it be soft for us![5] (*Knocking at the inn door:*) Hello, you in the inn! Hello, I say! Innkeeper or the devil! Won't anyone answer? What kind of establishment is this?

LEANDER: Why yell so loud when you've just started to call?

CRISPIN: Because it's a nasty thing to make people wait this way! (*Calling again, even louder:*) People! People of the inn! Oh, damn it all!

INNKEEPER (*within*): Who's there? What kind of yelling and behavior is this? You can't have been waiting long.

CRISPIN: It's been too long already! Those people were right who told us that this is a very wretched inn for members of the nobility.

Scene II

The above, the INNKEEPER, *and two* SERVANTS *who come out of the inn.*

INNKEEPER (*entering*): Be calm! This isn't a wayside tavern, but an elegant hostelry, and many a great lord has stayed here.

CRISPIN: I'd like to see who you're calling great lords. Riffraff of little importance! I can tell by looking at these servants, who can't recognize persons of quality, but just stand around like dunces without waiting on us.

INNKEEPER: My God, you've got a mouth on you!

LEANDER: This servant of mine always has to carry his zeal too far. Your inn is satisfactory for the short while I need to stay in it. Prepare a room for me at once, and another one for my servant, and let's not waste words.

---

5. The Spanish phrasing recalls the ancient Roman epitaph formula *Sit tibi terra levis* (May the earth lie lightly upon you).

HOSTELERO.—Perdonad, señor; si antes hubierais hablado . . . Siempre los señores han de ser más comedidos que sus criados.

CRISPÍN.—Es que este buen señor mío a todo se acomoda; pero yo sé lo que conviene a su servicio, y no he de pasar por cosa mal hecha. Conducidnos ya al aposento.

HOSTELERO.—¿No traéis bagaje alguno?

CRISPÍN.—¿Pensáis que nuestro pagaje es hatillo de soldado o de estudiante para traerlo a mano, ni que mi señor ha de traer aquí ocho carros, que tras nosotros vienen, ni que aquí ha de parar sino el tiempo preciso que conviene al secreto de los servicios que en esta ciudad le están encomendados? . . .

LEANDRO.—¿No callarás? ¿Qué secreto ha de haber contigo? ¡Pues voto a . . . , que si alguien me descubre por tu hablar sin medida! . . . (*Le amenaza y le pega con la espada.*)

CRISPÍN.—¡Valedme, que me matará! (*Corriendo.*)

HOSTELERO.—(*Interponiéndose entre* LEANDRO *y* CRISPÍN.) ¡Teneos, señor!

LEANDRO.—Dejad que le castigue, que no hay falta para mí como el hablar sin tino.

HOSTELERO.—¡No le castiguéis, señor!

LEANDRO.—¡Dejadme, dejadme, que no aprenderá nunca! (*Al ir a pegar a* CRISPÍN, *éste se esconde detrás del* HOSTELERO, *quien recibe los golpes.*)

CRISPÍN.—(*Quejándose.*) ¡Ay, ay, ay!

HOSTELERO.—¡Ay digo yo, que me dió de plano!

LEANDRO.—(*A* CRISPÍN.) Ve a lo que diste lugar: a que este infeliz fuera el golpeado. ¡Pídele perdón!

HOSTELERO.—No es menester. Yo le perdono gustoso. (*A los* CRIADOS.) ¿Qué hacéis ahí parados? Disponed los aposentos donde suele parar el embajador de Mantua y preparad comida para este caballero.

CRISPÍN.—Dejad que yo les advierta de todo, que cometerán mil torpezas y pagaré yo luego, que mi señor, como veis, no perdona falta . . . Soy con vosotros, muchachos . . . Y tened cuenta a quien servís, que la mayor fortuna o la mayor desdicha os entró por las puertas. (*Entran los* CRIADOS *y* CRISPÍN *en la hostería.*)

HOSTELERO.—(*A* LEANDRO.) ¿Y podéis decirme vuestro nombre, de dónde venís, y a qué propósito? . . .

LEANDRO.—(*Al ver salir a* CRISPÍN *de la hostería.*) Mi criado os lo

INNKEEPER: Pardon me, sir; if you had only spoken earlier. . . . Masters are always more polite than their servants.

CRISPIN: That's because my kindly master is willing to put up with anything; but I know what befits his service, and I'm not one to overlook a botched job. Come now, show us to our rooms!

INNKEEPER: Don't you have any luggage?

CRISPIN: Do you imagine that our luggage is some soldier's or student's knapsack that can be carried by hand, or that my master is going to bring here the eight wagons that are following us, or that he intends to stay here any longer than it takes him to carry out the secret mission that has been entrusted to him in this city?

LEANDER: Can't you keep still? How can there be any secrets with you around? By God, if someone finds out who I am because of your unending babble! . . . (*He threatens him and hits him with his sword.*)

CRISPIN: Help, or he'll kill me! (*Running away.*)

INNKEEPER (*interposing between* LEANDER *and* CRISPIN): Stop, my lord!

LEANDER: Let me punish him! To me, no fault is as bad as mindless chattering.

INNKEEPER: Don't punish him, sir!

LEANDER: Let me, let me, for he'll never learn! (*He goes to strike* CRISPIN, *who hides behind the* INNKEEPER, *and the* INNKEEPER *receives the blows.*)

CRISPIN (*moaning*): Ow! Ow! Ow!

INNKEEPER: I'm the one to say "Ow!" because he hit me with the flat of his sword!

LEANDER (*to* CRISPIN): Look what you've done! This poor man was the one who got hurt. Beg his pardon!

INNKEEPER: There's no need. I forgive him gladly. (*To the* SERVANTS:) Why are you standing stock-still? Prepare the rooms in which the ambassador from Mantua usually stays, and cook a meal for this gentleman.

CRISPIN: Let me advise them in all they do, or else they'll make all kinds of clumsy errors, and then I'll pay for it, because, as you see, my master doesn't forgive a mistake. . . . I'm with you, men. . . . And keep in mind whom you're serving, because either the greatest of good luck or the greatest misfortune has walked through your door! (*The* SERVANTS *and* CRISPIN *enter the inn.*)

INNKEEPER (*to* LEANDER): And can you tell me your name, where you're arriving from, and the purpose of your visit?

LEANDER (*seeing* CRISPIN *coming out of the inn*): My servant will

dirá . . . Y aprended a no importunarme con preguntas . . . (*Entra en la hostería.*)

CRISPÍN.—¡Buena la hicisteis! ¿Atreverse a preguntar a mi señor? Si os importa tenerle una hora siquiera en vuestra casa, no volváis a dirigirle la palabra.

HOSTELERO.—Sabed que hay Ordenanzas muy severas que así lo disponen.

CRISPÍN.—¡Veníos con Ordenanzas a mi señor! ¡Callad, callad, que no sabéis a quien tenéis en vuestra casa, y si lo supierais no diríais tantas impertinencias!

HOSTELERO.—Pero, ¿no he de saber siquiera? . . .

CRISPÍN.—¡Voto a . . . , que llamaré a mi señor y él os dirá lo que conviene, si no lo entendisteis! ¡Cuidad de que nada le falte y atendedle con vuestros cinco sentidos, que bien puede pesaros! ¿No sabéis conocer a las personas? ¿No visteis ya quién es mi señor? ¿Qué replicáis? ¡Vamos ya! (*Entra en la hostería empujando al* HOSTELERO.)

Escena III

ARLEQUÍN *y el* CAPITÁN, *que salen por la segunda izquierda*

ARLEQUÍN.—Vagando por los campos que rodean esta ciudad, lo mejor de ella sin duda alguna, creo que sin pensarlo hemos venido a dar frente a la hostería. ¡Animal de costumbre es el hombre! ¡Y dura costumbre la de alimentarse cada día!

CAPITÁN.—¡La dulce música de vuestros versos me distrajo de mis pensamientos! ¡Amable privilegio de los poetas!

ARLEQUÍN.—¡Que no les impide carecer de todo! Con temor llego a la hostería. ¿Consentirán hoy en fiarnos? ¡Válgame vuestra espada!

CAPITÁN.—¿Mi espada? Mi espada de soldado, como vuestro plectro de poeta, nada valen en esta ciudad de mercaderes y de negociantes . . . ¡Triste condición es la nuestra!

ARLEQUÍN.—Bien decís. No la sublime poesía, que sólo canta de nobles y elevados asuntos; ya ni sirve poner el ingenio a las plantas de los poderosos para elogiarlos o satirizarlos; alabanzas o diatribas no tienen valor para ellos; ni agradecen las unas ni temen las otras. El propio Aretino hubiera muerto de hambre en estos tiempos.

tell you. . . . And from here on, don't pester me with questions. . . . (*Enters the inn.*)

CRISPIN: A fine thing you've done! Daring to interrogate my master! If it means anything to you to retain him in your establishment for even an hour, don't address him again.

INNKEEPER: I'll have you know there are very strict local ordinances that require such information.

CRISPIN: Go tell my master about ordinances! Be still, be still, because you don't know whom you've got in your inn. If you knew, you wouldn't be so impertinent!

INNKEEPER: But can't I even find out?

CRISPIN: By God, I'll call my master, and he'll tell you all that's fit, if you didn't understand! Take care that he lacks for nothing, and wait on him with all your senses alert, or else you may be very sorry! Can't you distinguish among people? Haven't you realized who my master is? What's this back talk? Let's go! (*He enters the inn, pushing the* INNKEEPER *in front of him.*)

Scene III

HARLEQUIN *and the* CAPTAIN *enter from the second wing-space.*

HARLEQUIN: In our wanderings through the countryside that surrounds this city, which is its best feature without any doubt, I believe that we have unexpectedly arrived in front of the inn. What a creature of habit is man! And what a difficult habit it is to feed oneself every day!

CAPTAIN: The sweet music of your verses took my mind off my worries! A charming privilege that poets have!

HARLEQUIN: Which doesn't hinder them from being in total want! It's with apprehension that I arrive at the inn. Will they agree to give us credit today? May your sword help me!

CAPTAIN: My sword? My military sword, like your poetic plectrum, counts for nothing in this city of merchants and businessmen. . . . A sad lot is ours!

HARLEQUIN: You speak truly. They don't want sublime poetry, which sings of naught but noble and exalted subjects; it's no longer of any use to lay one's talent at the feet of the powerful to praise or lampoon them; neither eulogies nor diatribes have any meaning for them; they don't appreciate the former or fear the latter. Aretino[6] himself would have died of hunger in this day and age.

6. The Italian author Pietro Aretino (1492–1556), a fearless satirist.

CAPITÁN.—¿Y nosotros, decidme? Porque fuimos vencidos en las últimas guerras, más que por el enemigo poderoso, por esos indignos traficantes que nos gobiernan y nos enviaron a defender sus intereses sin fuerzas y sin entusiasmo, porque nadie combate con fe por lo que no estima; ellos, que no dieron uno de los suyos para soldado ni soltaron moneda sino a buen interés y a mejor cuenta, y apenas temieron verla perdida amenazaron con hacer causa con el enemigo, ahora nos culpan a nosotros y nos maltratan y nos menosprecian y quisieran ahorrarse la mísera soldada con que creen pagarnos, y de muy buena gana nos despedirían si no temieran que un día todos los oprimidos por sus maldades y tiranías se levantarán contra ellos. ¡Pobres de ellos si ese día nos acordamos de qué parte están la razón y la justicia!

ARLEQUÍN.—Si así fuera . . . , ese día me tendréis a vuestro lado.

CAPITÁN.—Con los poetas no hay que contar para nada, que es vuestro espíritu como el ópalo, que a cada luz hace diversos visos. Hoy os apasionáis por lo que nace y mañana por lo que muere; pero más inclinados sois a enamoraros de todo lo ruinoso por melancólico. Y como sois por lo regular poco madrugadores, más veces visteis morir el sol que amanecer el día, y más sabéis de sus ocasos que de sus auroras.

ARLEQUÍN.—No lo diréis por mí, que he visto amanecer muchas veces cuando no tenía dónde acostarme. ¿Y cómo queríais que cantara al día, alegre como alondra, si amanecía tan triste para mí? ¿Os decidís a probar fortuna?

CAPITÁN.—¡Qué remedio! Sentémonos, y sea lo que disponga nuestro buen hostelero.

ARLEQUÍN.—¡Hola! ¡Eh! ¿Quién sirve? (*Llamando en la hostería.*)

Escena IV

DICHOS, *el* HOSTELERO. *Después los* MOZOS, LEANDRO *y* CRISPÍN, *que salen a su tiempo de la hostería*

HOSTELERO.—¡Ah caballeros! ¿Sois vosotros? Mucho lo siento, pero hoy no puedo servir a nadie en mi hostería.

CAPITÁN.—¿Y por qué causa, si puede saberse?

CAPTAIN: Tell me, what about us? Because we were beaten in the latest wars,[7] not so much by the powerful enemy as by those shameless traffickers who govern us and who sent us to defend their interests without sufficient manpower or enthusiasm (for no one fights faithfully for that which he doesn't esteem)—those same men who failed to hand over one of their own kind to serve in the army and didn't unhand a penny except at high interest and for even higher profit, those who no sooner feared to see the war lost than they threatened to ally themselves with the enemy—*they* now blame *us* and treat us badly and belittle us and would like to save even the wretched pay with which they think they're remunerating us; and they'd be very glad to discharge us, except they're afraid that some day all those oppressed by their crimes and tyranny may rise up against them. Woe to them if, on that day, we remember on what side reason and justice stand!

HARLEQUIN: If it came to that . . . , on that day you'd have me on your side.

CAPTAIN: Poets can't be counted on for anything, because your minds are like opal: it looks different with every change of lighting. Today you're all agog over things that are being born, and tomorrow for things that are dying; but you're more inclined to become enamored of everything that's dilapidated for the sake of its melancholy. And since you're not normally early risers, you've seen the sun die more often than you've seen the day break, and you know more about its sunsets than its dawns.

HARLEQUIN: You can't say that about me, because I've seen the day break many times when I had no place to sleep. And how can you ask me to sing about the day, merry as a lark, when it has dawned so unhappily for me? Have you made up your mind to try your luck?

CAPTAIN: What else can I do? Let's sit down, and accept whatever our kind innkeeper determines to do.

HARLEQUIN: Hello in there! Hey! Service, please! (*Calling into the inn.*)

Scene IV

The above, the INNKEEPER. *Later, the* SERVANTS, LEANDER, *and* CRISPIN, *who come out of the inn at the time indicated.*

INNKEEPER: Oh, gentlemen! It's you? I'm very sorry, but today I can't serve anyone in my hostelry.

CAPTAIN: And why not, if I may ask?

7. Very possibly a reference to the Spanish-American War of 1898, in which Spain lost colonies and prestige.

HOSTELERO.—¡Lindo desahogo es el vuestro en preguntarlo! ¿Pensáis que a mí me fía nadie lo que en mi casa se gasta?

CAPITÁN.—¡Ah! ¿Es ése el motivo? ¿Y no somos personas de crédito a quien puede fiarse?

HOSTELERO.—Para mí, no. Y como nunca pensé cobrar, para favor ya fué bastante; conque así, hagan merced de no volver por mi casa.

ARLEQUÍN.—¿Creéis que todo es dinero en este bajo mundo? ¿Contáis por nada las ponderaciones que de vuestra casa hicimos en todas partes? ¡Hasta un soneto os tengo dedicado y en él celebro vuestras perdices estofadas y vuestros pasteles de liebre! . . . Y en cuanto al señor Capitán, tened por seguro que él solo sostendrá contra un ejército el buen nombre de vuestra casa. ¿Nada vale esto? ¡Todo ha de ser moneda contante en el mundo!

HOSTELERO.—¡No estoy para burlas! No he menester de vuestros sonetos ni de la espada del señor Capitán, que mejor pudiera emplearla.

CAPITÁN.—¡Voto a . . . , que sí la emplearé escarmentando a un pícaro! (*Amenazándole y pegándole con la espada.*)

HOSTELERO.—(*Gritando.*) ¿Qué es esto? ¿Contra mí? ¡Favor! ¡Justicia!

ARLEQUÍN.—(*Conteniendo al* CAPITÁN.) ¡No os perdáis por tan ruin sujeto!

CAPITÁN.—He de matarle. (*Pegándole.*)

HOSTELERO.—¡Favor! ¡Justicia!

MOZOS.—(*Saliendo de la hostería.*) ¡Que matan a nuestro amo!

HOSTELERO.—¡Socorredme!

CAPITÁN.—¡No dejaré uno!

HOSTELERO.—¿No vendrá nadie?

LEANDRO.—(*Saliendo con* CRISPÍN.) ¿Qué alboroto es éste?

CRISPÍN.—¿En lugar donde mi señor se hospeda? ¿No hay sosiego posible en vuestra casa? Yo traeré a la Justicia, que pondrá orden en ello.

HOSTELERO.—¡Esto ha de ser mi ruina! ¡Con tan gran señor en mi casa!

ARLEQUÍN.—¿Quién es él?

HOSTELERO.—¡No oséis preguntarlo!

CAPITÁN.—Perdonad, señor, si turbamos vuestro reposo; pero este ruin hostelero . . .

HOSTELERO.—No fué mía la culpa, señor, sino de estos desvergonzados . . .

CAPITÁN.—¿A mí desvergonzado? ¡No miraré nada! . . .

INNKEEPER: You're pretty brazen to be asking that! Do you think anyone gives me the provisions I need on credit?

CAPTAIN: Aha! So that's the reason! Aren't we substantial people who are eligible for credit?

INNKEEPER: Not to me. And since I never expected to get my money back, I've given away enough free meals now; therefore, be so good as not to return to my establishment.

HARLEQUIN: Do you think money is everything in this vile world? Do you count as nothing the praises we have heaped on your inn everywhere we go? I've even dedicated a sonnet to you, in which I extol your stewed partridges and your hare pies! . . . And as for the Captain here, be assured that, singlehanded, he will uphold the good repute of your inn against a whole army. Does that have no value? Everything in this world must be cash!

INNKEEPER: I'm in no mood for jokes! I don't need your sonnets or the Captain's sword, which he could put to better use.

CAPTAIN: By God, I'll use it to teach a scoundrel a lesson! (*Threatening him and beating him with the sword.*)

INNKEEPER (*yelling*): What's this? Beating *me*? Help! Police!

HARLEQUIN (*restraining the* CAPTAIN): Don't get into trouble on account of this low creature!

CAPTAIN: I'm going to kill him. (*Striking him.*)

INNKEEPER: Help! Police!

SERVANTS (*coming out of the inn*): Look, they're killing our master!

INNKEEPER: Help me!

CAPTAIN: I won't leave one of them alive!

INNKEEPER: Won't anybody come?

LEANDER (*entering with* CRISPIN): What's all this uproar?

CRISPIN: In a place where my master is lodging? Isn't it possible to have any peace in your inn? I'll call the police, and they'll settle the matter.

INNKEEPER: This will be my ruination! With such a noble lord in my establishment!

HARLEQUIN: Who is he?

INNKEEPER: Don't dare to ask!

CAPTAIN: Forgive us, sir, if we're disturbing your rest; but this vile innkeeper . . .

INNKEEPER: It wasn't my fault, sir, these shameless fellows are to blame . . .

CAPTAIN: I shameless? Now, no holds barred! . . .

CRISPÍN.—¡Alto, señor Capitán, que aquí tenéis quien satisfaga vuestros agravios, si los tenéis de este hombre!

HOSTELERO.—Figuraos que ha más de un mes que comen a mi costa sin soltar blanca, y porque me negué hoy a servirles se vuelven contra mí.

ARLEQUÍN.—Yo no, que todo lo llevo con paciencia.

CAPITÁN.—¿Y es razón que a un soldado no se le haga crédito?

ARLEQUÍN.—¿Y es razón que en nada se estime un soneto con estrambote que compuse a sus perdices estofadas y a sus pasteles de liebre? . . . Todo por fe, que no los probé nunca, sino carnero y potajes.

CRISPÍN.—Estos dos nobles señores dicen muy bien, y es indignidad tratar de ese modo a un poeta y a un soldado.

ARLEQUÍN.—¡Ah señor, sois un alma grande!

CRISPÍN.—Yo no. Mi señor, aquí presente; que como tan gran señor, nada hay para él en el mundo como un poeta y un soldado.

LEANDRO.—Cierto.

CRISPÍN.—Y estad seguros de que mientras él pare en esta ciudad no habéis de carecer de nada, y cuanto gasto hagáis aquí corre de su cuenta.

LEANDRO.—Cierto.

CRISPÍN.—¡Y mírese mucho el hostelero en trataros como corresponde!

HOSTELERO.—¡Señor!

CRISPÍN.—Y no seáis tan avaro de vuestras perdices ni de vuestras empanadas de gato, que no es razón que un poeta como el señor Arlequín hable por sueño de cosas tan palpables . . .

ARLEQUÍN.—¿Conocéis mi nombre?

CRISPÍN.—Yo no; pero mi señor, como tan gran señor, conoce a cuantos poetas existen y existieron, siempre que sean dignos de ese nombre.

LEANDRO.—Cierto.

CRISPÍN.—Y ninguno tan grande como vos, señor Arlequín; y cada vez que pienso que aquí no se os ha guardado todo el respeto que merecéis . . .

HOSTELERO.—Perdonad, señor. Yo les serviré como mandáis, y basta que seáis su fiador . . .

CAPITÁN.—Señor, si en algo puedo serviros . . .

CRISPÍN.—¿Es poco servicio el conoceros? ¡Glorioso Capitán, digno de ser cantado por este solo poeta! . . .

ARLEQUÍN.—¡Señor!

CAPITÁN.—¡Señor!

CRISPIN: Halt, Captain! Here you have the man to redress your wrongs, if this fellow has inflicted any on you!

INNKEEPER: Just imagine: for more than a month now, they've been dining at my expense without paying a cent, and because I refused to serve them today, they turned on me.

HARLEQUIN: Not I, for I bear everything patiently.

CAPTAIN: Is it right not to extend credit to a soldier?

HARLEQUIN: Is it right to disregard a tailed sonnet which I wrote in honor of his stewed partridges and hare pies? . . . And all on faith, because I've never tasted them; all I ever got was mutton or vegetable casseroles.

CRISPIN: These two noble gentlemen are perfectly right, and it's an indignity to treat a poet and a soldier this way.

HARLEQUIN: Ah, sir, you have a lofty soul!

CRISPIN: Not I: my master, whom you see here. Being such a great lord, he considers nothing in the world equal to a poet and a soldier.

LEANDER: Right!

CRISPIN: And be assured that, as long as he remains in this city, you shall want for nothing, and the entire tab you run up here will be added to his bill.

LEANDER: Right!

CRISPIN: And the innkeeper is to take pains to treat you as you deserve!

INNKEEPER: Sir!

CRISPIN: And don't be so stingy with your partridges and your cat turnovers, because it's unjust for a poet like Mr. Harlequin merely to dream about things that are so palpable . . .

HARLEQUIN: You know my name?

CRISPIN: Not I; but my master, being such a great lord, knows all the poets who exist or have existed, provided that they were worthy of that title.

LEANDER: Right!

CRISPIN: And none is as great as you, Mr. Harlequin; and every time I recall that you weren't given all the respect here that's due to you . . .

INNKEEPER: Forgive me, sir. I'll serve them as you order me to; it's enough for me that you vouch for them . . .

CAPTAIN: Sir, if I can do you any service . . .

CRISPIN: Isn't your acquaintance sufficient service? Illustrious Captain, worthy of being sung by this poet alone! . . .

HARLEQUIN: Sir!

CAPTAIN: Sir!

ARLEQUÍN.—¿Y os son conocidos mis versos?

CRISPÍN.—¿Cómo conocidos? ¡Olvidados los tengo! ¿No es vuestro aquel soneto admirable que empieza:

"La dulce mano que acaricia y mata"?

ARLEQUÍN.—¿Cómo decís?

CRISPÍN.—"La dulce mano que acaricia y mata."

ARLEQUÍN.—¿Ése decís? No, no es mío ese soneto.

CRISPÍN.—Pues merece ser vuestro. Y de vos, Capitán, ¿quién no conoce las hazañas? ¿No fuisteis el que solo con veinte hombres asaltó el castillo de las Peñas Rojas en la famosa batalla de los Campos Negros?

CAPITÁN.—¿Sabéis? . . .

CRISPÍN.—¿Cómo si sabemos? ¡Oh! ¡Cuántas veces se lo oí referir a mi señor entusiasmado! Veinte hombres, veinte y vos delante, y desde el castillo . . . , ¡bum!, ¡bum!, ¡bum!, disparos y bombardas y pez hirviente, y demonios encendidos . . . ¡Y los veinte hombres como un solo hombre y vos delante! Y los de arriba . . . , ¡bum!, ¡bum!, ¡bum! Y los tambores . . . , ¡ran, rataplán, plan! Y los clarines . . . , ¡tararí, tararí, tararí! . . . Y vosotros sólo con vuestra espada y vos sin espada . . . , ¡ris, ris, ris!, golpe aquí, golpe allí . . . , una cabeza, un brazo . . . (*Empieza a golpes con la espada, dándoles de plano al* HOSTELERO *y a los* MOZOS.)

MOZO.—¡Ay, ay!

HOSTELERO.—¡Téngase, que se apasiona como si pasara!

CRISPÍN.—¿Cómo si me apasiono? Siempre sentí yo el *animus belli.*

CAPITÁN.—No parece sino que os hallasteis presente.

CRISPÍN.—Oírselo referir a mi señor es como verlo, mejor que verlo. ¡Y a un soldado así, al héroe de las Peñas Rojas en los Campos Negros, se le trata de esa manera! . . . ¡Ah! Gran suerte fué que mi señor se hallase presente, y que negocios de importancia le hayan traído a esta ciudad, donde él hará que se os trate con respeto, como merecéis . . . ¡Un poeta tan alto, un tan gran capitán! (*A los* MOZOS.) ¡Pronto! ¿Qué hacéis ahí como estafermos? Servidles de lo mejor que haya en vuestra casa, y ante todo una botella del mejor vino, que mi señor quiere beber con estos caballeros, y lo tendrá a gloria . . . ¿Qué hacéis ahí? ¡Pronto!

HOSTELERO.—¡Voy, voy! ¡No he librado de mala! (*Se va con los* MOZOS *a la hostería.*)

HARLEQUIN: And you're familiar with my poetry?

CRISPIN: Familiar?! I've known it so long that I'm forgetting some! Didn't you write that admirable sonnet which begins:

"That velvet hand which kills as it caresses"?

HARLEQUIN: Say it again?

CRISPIN: "That velvet hand which kills as it caresses."

HARLEQUIN: You mean that one? No, I didn't write that sonnet.

CRISPIN: Well, it deserves to be by you. And you, Captain, who doesn't know your exploits? Weren't you the one who, with only twenty men, attacked the castle of the Red Cliffs during the famous battle of the Black Fields?

CAPTAIN: You know that?! . . .

CRISPIN: I'll say we know! Oh, how often I've heard my master tell about it enthusiastically! Twenty men, twenty with you at their head, and from the castle: boom, boom, boom, gunshots and bombards and boiling pitch, and blazing missiles . . . And the twenty men like a single man, and you leading them! And the enemy above you: boom, boom, boom! And the drums: rat-a-tat-tat! And the bugles: tarantara! And you alone with your sword, and you without your sword: swish, swish, swish! A blow here, a blow there . . . a head, an arm . . . (*He begins to deal blows with his sword, beating the* INNKEEPER *and the* SERVANTS *with the flat of it.*)

SERVANT: Ow! Ow!

INNKEEPER: Stop! You're as excited as if it were going on right now!

CRISPIN: Of course, I'm excited. I've always felt the *animus belli*.[8]

CAPTAIN: You tell it exactly as if you had been there.

CRISPIN: Hearing my master narrate it is just like seeing it—even better! And that a soldier like this, the hero of the Red Cliffs in the Black Fields, should be treated this way! . . . Ah, it was a great stroke of luck that my master was on hand, having been brought to this city by affairs of importance; here he'll see that you're treated with respect, as you deserve. . . . So lofty a poet, so great a captain! (*To the* SERVANTS:) Make it snappy! Why are you standing there like dumbbells? Serve them the best food you have in your inn, and above all a bottle of your best wine, because my master wishes to drink with these gentlemen, and he'll consider it an honor. . . . Why are you still here? Get a move on!

INNKEEPER: I'm going, I'm going! Now, wasn't that a close call! (*He returns to the inn with the* SERVANTS.)

8. Latin for "warlike spirit."

ARLEQUÍN.—¡Ah señor! ¿Cómo agradeceros? . . .

CAPITÁN.—¿Cómo pagaros?

CRISPÍN.—¡Nadie hable aquí de pagar, que es palabra que ofende! Sentaos, sentaos, que para mi señor, que a tantos príncipes y grandes ha sentado a su mesa, será éste el mayor orgullo.

LEANDRO.—Cierto.

CRISPÍN.—Mi señor no es de muchas palabras; pero, como veis, esas pocas son otras tantas sentencias llenas de sabiduría.

ARLEQUÍN.—En todo muestra su grandeza.

CAPITÁN.—No sabéis cómo conforta nuestro abatido espíritu hallar un gran señor como vos, que así nos considera.

CRISPÍN.—Esto no es nada, que yo sé que mí señor no se contenta con tan poco y será capaz de llevaros consigo y colocaros en tan alto estado . . .

LEANDRO.—(*Aparte a* CRISPÍN.) No te alargues en palabras, Crispín . . .

CRISPÍN.—Mi señor no gusta de palabras, pero ya le conoceréis por las obras.

HOSTELERO.—(*Saliendo con los* MOZOS, *que traen las viandas y ponen la mesa.*) Aquí está el vino . . . , y la comida.

CRISPÍN.—¡Beban, beban y coman y no se priven de nada, que mi señor corre con todo, y si algo os falta, no dudéis de decirlo, que mi señor pondrá orden en ello, que el hostelero es dado a descuidarse!

HOSTELERO.—No, por cierto; pero comprenderéis . . .

CRISPÍN.—No digáis palabra, que diréis una impertinencia.

CAPITÁN.—¡A vuestra salud!

LEANDRO.—¡A la vuestra, señores! ¡Por el más grande poeta y el mejor soldado!

ARLEQUÍN.—¡Por el más noble señor!

CAPITÁN.—¡Por el más generoso!

CRISPÍN.—Y yo también he de beber, aunque sea atrevimiento. Por este día grande entre todos que juntó al más alto poeta, al más valiente capitán, al más noble señor y al más leal criado . . . Y permitid que mi señor se despida, que los negocios que le traen a esta ciudad no admiten demora.

LEANDRO.—Cierto.

CRISPÍN.—¿No faltaréis a presentarle vuestros respetos cada día?

ARLEQUÍN.—Y a cada hora; y he de juntar a todos los músicos y poetas de mi amistad para festejarle con músicas y canciones.

CAPITÁN.—Y yo he de traer a toda mi compañía con antorchas y luminarias.

HARLEQUIN: Oh, sir! How can I thank you? . . .

CAPTAIN: How can I repay you?

CRISPIN: Let there be no talk of payment, which is an insulting expression! Be seated, be seated, because my master, who has seated so many princes and grandees at his table, will consider this his greatest pride.

LEANDER: Right!

CRISPIN: My master is a man of few words, but, as you see, those few are all maxims full of wisdom.

HARLEQUIN: He displays his greatness in everything he does.

CAPTAIN: You don't know how it comforts our depressed spirits to come across a great lord like you who esteems us so highly.

CRISPIN: That's nothing; I know that my master won't be satisfied with so little, and that he may even take you along and raise you to such high rank . . .

LEANDER (*aside to* CRISPIN): Don't get carried away, Crispin!

CRISPIN: My master isn't fond of talk; you'll get to know him by his deeds.

INNKEEPER (*entering with the* SERVANTS, *who are carrying the food and setting the table*): Here's the wine . . . and the meal.

CRISPIN: Drink! Eat and drink, and don't begrudge yourselves a thing, because my master is standing surety for everything, and if you lack anything, don't hesitate to say so, and my master will procure it—because the innkeeper is inclined to be careless!

INNKEEPER: No, indeed! But you'll surely understand . . .

CRISPIN: Don't say a word, or you'll say something impertinent!

CAPTAIN: To your health!

LEANDER: To yours, gentlemen! To the greatest poet and the best soldier!

HARLEQUIN: To the most noble lord!

CAPTAIN: And the most generous!

CRISPIN: And I'll drink, too, though it may be presumptuous of me. To this great day of days, which has brought together the most exalted poet, the most valiant captain, the most noble lord, and the most loyal servant! And allow my master to take his leave, because the business that brings him to this city brooks no delay.

LEANDER: Right!

CRISPIN: You won't fail to pay him your respects daily?

HARLEQUIN: Even hourly! And I'm going to assemble all the musicians and poets I'm friends with, to entertain him with music and singing.

CAPTAIN: And I'm going to bring my entire company with torches and lanterns.

LEANDRO.—Ofenderéis mi modestia . . .

CRISPÍN.—Y ahora comed, bebed . . . ¡Pronto! Servid a estos señores . . . (*Aparte al* CAPITÁN.) Entre nosotros . . . , ¿estaréis sin blanca?

CAPITÁN.—¿Qué hemos de deciros?

CRISPÍN.—¡No digáis más! (*Al* HOSTELERO.) ¡Eh! ¡Aquí! Entregaréis a estos caballeros cuarenta o cincuenta escudos por encargo de mi señor y de parte suya . . . ¡No dejéis de cumplir sus órdenes!

HOSTELERO.—¡Descuidad! ¿Cuarenta o cincuenta, decís?

CRISPÍN.—Poned sesenta . . . ¡Caballeros, salud!

CAPITÁN.—¡Viva el más grande caballero!

ARLEQUÍN.—¡Viva!

CRISPÍN.—¡Decid ¡viva! también vosotros, gente incivil!

HOSTELERO y MOZOS.—¡Viva!

CRISPÍN.—¡Viva el más alto poeta y el mayor soldado!

TODOS.—¡Viva!

LEANDRO.—(*Aparte a* CRISPÍN.) ¿Qué locuras son éstas, Crispín, y cómo saldremos de ellas?

CRISPÍN.—Como entramos. Ya lo ves; la poesía y las armas son nuestras . . . ¡Adelante! ¡Sigamos la conquista del mundo! (*Todos se hacen saludos y reverencias, y* LEANDRO *y* CRISPÍN *se van por la segunda izquierda. El* CAPITÁN *y* ARLEQUÍN *se disponen a comer los asados que les han preparado el* HOSTELERO *y los* MOZOS *que los sirven.*)

Mutación

LEANDER: I'm too modest for all that. . . .

CRISPIN: And now eat, drink . . . Quick! Serve these gentlemen! . . . (*Aside to the* CAPTAIN:) Just between ourselves . . . are you short of cash?

CAPTAIN: What can we tell you?

CRISPIN: Say no more! (*To the* INNKEEPER:) Hey! Come here! You are to hand over to these gentlemen forty or fifty crowns on my master's account, and as coming from him. . . . Don't fail to carry out his orders!

INNKEEPER: Don't worry! Forty or fifty, you said?

CRISPIN: Make it sixty. . . . Gentlemen, your health!

CAPTAIN: Long live the greatest gentleman!

HARLEQUIN: Long may he live!

CRISPIN: You say "Long may he live," too, you discourteous people!

INNKEEPER and SERVANTS: Long may he live!

CRISPIN: Here's to the loftiest poet and the greatest soldier!

ALL: Long may they live!

LEANDER (*aside to* CRISPIN): What's all this madness, Crispin, and how will we ever get out of it?

CRISPIN: The same way we got in. Now you see: poetry and weaponry belong to us. . . . Forward! Let's pursue the conquest of the world! (*They all take leave with bows, and* LEANDER *and* CRISPIN *exit into the second wing-space, left. The* CAPTAIN *and* HARLEQUIN *prepare to eat the roasts that have been cooked for them by the* INNKEEPER *and the* SERVANTS, *who wait on them.*)

Change of scene.

Cuadro segundo

Jardín con fachada de un pabellón, con puerta practicable en primer término izquierda. Es de noche

Escena I

DOÑA SIRENA *y* COLOMBINA, *saliendo del pabellón*

SIRENA.—¿No hay para perder el juicio, Colombina? ¡Que una dama se vea en trance tan afrentoso por gente baja y descomedida! ¿Cómo te atreviste a volver a mi presencia con tales razones?

COLOMBINA.—¿Y no habíais de saberlo?

SIRENA.—¡Morir me estaría mejor! ¿Y todos te dijeron lo mismo?

COLOMBINA.—Uno por uno, como lo oísteis . . . El sastre, que no os enviará el vestido mientras no le paguéis todo lo adeudado.

SIRENA.—¡El insolente! ¡El salteador de caminos! ¡Cuando es él quien me debe todo su crédito en esta ciudad, que hasta emplearlo yo en el atavío de mi persona no supo lo que era vestir damas!

COLOMBINA.—Y los cocineros y los músicos y los criados todos dijeron lo mismo: que no servirán esta noche en la fiesta si no les pagáis por adelantado.

SIRENA.—¡Los sayones! ¡Los forajidos! ¡Cuándo se vió tanta insolencia en gente nacida para servirnos! ¿Es que ya no se paga más que con dinero? ¿Es que ya sólo se estima el dinero en el mundo? ¡Triste de la que se ve como yo, sin el amparo de un marido, ni de parientes, ni de allegados masculinos! . . . Que una mujer sola nada vale en el mundo, por noble y virtuosa que sea. ¡Oh tiempos de perdición! ¡Tiempos del Apocalipsis! ¡El Anticristo debe ser llegado!

COLOMBINA.—Nunca os vi tan apocada. Os desconozco. De mayores apuros supisteis salir adelante.

Second Tableau

Garden, with the facade of a pavilion, with a practicable door downstage, left. It is nighttime.

Scene I

MADAM SIRENA *and* COLUMBINE *enter from the pavilion.*

SIRENA: Couldn't a person just lose her mind, Columbine? For a lady to find herself in such an insulting position because of low, impolite people! How did you dare to come back to me with such a message?

COLUMBINE: And shouldn't you have expected it?

SIRENA: It would be better for me to die! Everyone told you the same thing?

COLUMBINE: Each and every one, just as I've reported. . . . The tailor says he won't send you the gown until you pay him everything you owe him.

SIRENA: Insolent man! Highway robber! When it's *he* who owes to *me* all the reputation he has in this city!—because, before I employed him to create my wardrobe, he had no idea what it meant to make clothes for ladies!

COLUMBINE: And the cooks and the musicians and the waiters all said the same: they won't serve you at your party tonight if you don't pay them in advance.

SIRENA: Those hangmen! Those outlaws! When was such insolence ever seen in people who were born to wait on us? Is money the only means of payment that still exists? Is money now the only thing esteemed in the world? Unhappy the woman who finds herself in my situation, without the protection of a husband or relatives or male connections! . . . A solitary woman counts for nothing in society, however noble and virtuous she may be. Oh, these ruinous times! Apocalyptic times! The Antichrist must have come!

COLUMBINE: I've never seen you so beaten down. I don't recognize you. You've been able to get out of worse messes.

SIRENA.—Eran otros tiempos, Colombina. Contaba yo entonces con mi juventud y con mi belleza como poderosos aliados. Príncipes y grandes señores rendíanse a mis plantas.

COLOMBINA.—En cambio, no sería tanta vuestra experiencia y conocimiento del mundo como ahora. Y en cuanto a vuestra belleza, nunca estuvo tan en su punto, podéis creerlo.

SIRENA.—¡Deja lisonjas! ¡Cuándo me vería yo de este modo si fuera la doña Sirena de mis veinte!

COLOMBINA.—¿Años queréis decir?

SIRENA.—Pues, ¿qué pensaste? ¡Y qué diré de ti, que aún no los cumpliste y no sabes aprovecharlo! ¡Nunca lo creyera, cuando al verme tan sola, de criada, te adopté por sobrina! ¡Si en vez de malograr tu juventud enamorándote de ese Arlequín, ese poeta que nada puede ofrecer sino versos y músicas, supieras emplearte mejor, no nos veríamos en tan triste caso!

COLOMBINA.—¿Qué queréis? Aún soy demasiado joven para resignarme a ser amada y no corresponder. Y si he de adiestrarme en hacer padecer por mi amor, necesito saber antes cómo se padece cuando se ama. Yo sabré desquitarme. Aún no cumplí los veinte años. No me creáis con tan poco juicio que piense en casarme con Arlequín.

SIRENA.—No me fío de ti, que eres muy caprichosa y siempre te dejaste llevar de la fantasía. Pero pensemos en lo que ahora importa. ¿Qué haremos en tan gran apuro? No tardarán en acudir mis convidados, todos personas de calidad y de importancia, y entre ellas el señor Polichinela con su esposa y su hija, que por muchas razones me importan más que todos. Ya sabes cómo frecuentan esta casa algunos caballeros nobilísimos, pero, como yo, harto deslucidos en su nobleza, por falta de dinero. Para cualquiera de ellos, la hija del señor Polichinela, con su riquísima dote, y el gran caudal que ha de heredar a la muerte de su padre, puede ser un partido muy ventajoso. Muchos son los que la pretenden. En favor de todos ellos interpongo yo mi buena amistad con el señor Polichinela y su esposa. Cualquiera que sea el favorecido, yo sé que ha de corresponder con largueza a mis buenos oficios, que de todos me hice firmar una obligación para asegurarme. Ya no me quedan otros medios que estas mediaciones para reponer en algo mi patrimonio; si de camino algún rico comerciante o mercader se prendara de ti . . . , ¿quién sabe? . . . , aún podía ser esta casa lo que fué en otro tiempo. Pero si esta noche la insolencia de esa gente trasciende, si no puedo ofrecer la fiesta . . . ¡No quiero pensarlo . . . , que será mi ruina!

SIRENA: Those were other days, Columbine. At that time I could rely on my youth and beauty as mighty allies. Princes and great lords fell at my feet.

COLUMBINE: On the other hand, you couldn't have had the experience and the knowledge of society that you have now. And as for your beauty, it has never been at such a peak, take my word for it.

SIRENA: Stop flattering me! How would I find myself in these difficulties if I were still the Madam Sirena of twenty?

COLUMBINE: You mean: *age* twenty?

SIRENA: Of course! Did you think: twenty men? And what shall I say about you? You aren't even that old, and you don't know how to profit by your youth! I'd never have believed it when, finding myself so all alone, I took you, my servant, and adopted you as my niece! If, instead of wasting your youth by falling in love with that Harlequin, a poet who can offer you nothing but verses and music, you knew how to make better use of yourself, we wouldn't find ourselves in such a deplorable situation!

COLUMBINE: What do you want? I'm still too young to resign myself to be loved and not to reciprocate. And if I've got to train myself to make men suffer for love of me, I need to know first how people suffer when they're in love. I'll be able to make good my losses. I'm not yet twenty. Don't think I have so little sense that I intend to marry Harlequin.

SIRENA: I don't trust you, because you're very capricious and you've always let yourself be guided by your fancy. But let's think about what's important right now. What are we to do in such a great emergency? My guests will be arriving before long, all persons of quality and importance, among them Mr. Punchinello with his wife and daughter, who for many reasons are more important to me than all the rest. You know that my home is frequented by some gentlemen of the highest nobility, though, like me, they're greatly tarnished in their nobility for lack of money. For any one of them Mr. Punchinello's daughter, with her enormous dowry and the great fortune she is to inherit when her father dies, could be a most advantageous match. Many men seek her hand. In favor of all of them I intercede with Mr. Punchinello and his wife on the strength of my close friendship with the family. Whoever is the husband selected, I know he'll compensate my good offices generously, because I had all of them sign an agreement to that effect, to put my mind at ease. Now I have no means other than these mediations to restore my finances to some extent; if, at the same time, some rich businessman or merchant should take a liking to you . . . who knows? This house might still be what it was in the past. But if that rabble's insolence were to leak out tonight, if I'm unable to give the party . . . It's unthinkable . . . , it will be my ruin!

COLOMBINA.—No paséis cuidado. Con qué agasajarlos no ha de faltar. Y en cuanto a músicos y a criados, el señor Arlequín, que por algo es poeta y para algo está enamorado de mí, sabrá improvisarlo todo. Él conoce a muchos truhanes de buen humor que han de prestarse a todo. Ya veréis, no faltará nada, y vuestros convidados dirán que no asistieron en su vida a tan maravillosa fiesta.

SIRENA.—¡Ay Colombina! Si eso fuera, ¡cuánto ganarías en mi afecto! Corre en busca de tu poeta . . . No hay que perder tiempo.

COLOMBINA.—¿Mi poeta? Del otro lado de estos jardines pasea, de seguro, aguardando una seña mía . . .

SIRENA.—No será bien que asista a vuestra entrevista, que yo no debo rebajarme en solicitar tales favores . . . A tu cargo lo dejo. ¡Que nada falte para la fiesta, y yo sabré recompensar a todos; que esta estrechez angustiosa de ahora no puede durar siempre . . . , o no sería yo doña Sirena!

COLOMBINA.—Todo se compondrá. Id descuidada. (*Vase* DOÑA SIRENA *por el pabellón.*)

Escena II

COLOMBINA. *Después* CRISPÍN, *que sale por la segunda derecha*

COLOMBINA.—(*Dirigiéndose a la segunda derecha y llamando.*) ¡Arlequín! ¡Arlequín! (*Al ver salir a* CRISPÍN.) ¡No es él!

CRISPÍN.—No temáis, hermosa Colombina, amada del más soberano ingenio, que por ser raro poeta en todo, no quiso extremar en sus versos las ponderaciones de vuestra belleza. Si de lo vivo a lo pintado fué siempre diferencia, es toda en esta ocasión ventaja de lo vivo, ¡con ser tal la pintura!

COLOMBINA.—Y vos, ¿sois también poeta, o sólo cortesano y lisonjero?

CRISPÍN.—Soy el mejor amigo de vuestro enamorado Arlequín, aunque sólo de hoy le conozco, pero tales pruebas tuvo de mi amistad en tan corto tiempo. Mi mayor deseo fué el de saludaros, y el señor Arlequín no anduviera tan discreto en complacerme a no fiar tanto de mi amistad, que sin ella, fuera ponerme a riesgo de amaros sólo con haberme puesto en ocasión de veros.

COLOMBINA.—El señor Arlequín fiaba tanto en el amor que le tengo como en la amistad que le tenéis. No pongáis todo el mérito de

COLUMBINE: Don't worry about it. There won't be any lack of food to offer them. And as for musicians and waiters, Mr. Harlequin, who isn't a poet for nothing, and isn't in love with me for nothing, will be able to improvise it all. He knows many good-natured rogues who'll lend themselves to anything. You'll see, nothing will be lacking, and your guests will say they never attended such a marvelous party in their life.

SIRENA: Ah, Columbine! If all of that really happens, how you would rise in my affections! Run and find that poet of yours. . . . There's no time to lose.

COLUMBINE: That poet of mine? He's surely pacing to and fro on the other side of this garden, awaiting a signal from me. . . .

SIRENA: It wouldn't do for me to be present at your meeting, because I mustn't lower myself by requesting such favors. . . . I leave it to you. Let nothing be lacking for the party, and I'll manage to repay everyone, because this painful poverty I'm suffering now can't last forever . . . , or else my name isn't Madam Sirena!

COLUMBINE: Everything will be straightened out. Go and don't worry. (MADAM SIRENA *exits by way of the pavilion.*)

Scene II

COLUMBINE, *then* CRISPIN, *who enters from the second wing-space, right.*

COLUMBINE (*facing the second wing-space, right, and calling*): Harlequin! Harlequin! (*Seeing* CRISPIN *enter:*) It's someone else!

CRISPIN: Have no fear, lovely Columbine, beloved by the most sovereign intellect, who, because he is an excellent poet in all ways, refrained from exaggerating your praises in his verses. If there's always a difference between a portrait and its subject, in this case the advantage is completely on the side of the living subject, however beautiful the painting!

COLUMBINE: And are you a poet, too, or merely a courtier and flatterer?

CRISPIN: I'm the best friend of your lover Harlequin, though I met him only today—but he's had mighty proofs of my friendship in that brief period. My greatest desire was to meet you, and Mr. Harlequin wouldn't have been very prudent in granting me that pleasure, were it not that he trusted so much in my friendship; otherwise, it would have meant exposing me to the risk of loving you, merely by giving me the opportunity to set eyes on you.

COLUMBINE: Mr. Harlequin trusted just as much in my love for him as in your friendship toward him. Don't take all the credit for yourself,

vuestra parte, que es tan necia presunción perdonar la vida a los hombres como el corazón a las mujeres.

CRISPÍN.—Ahora advierto que no sois tan peligrosa al que os ve como al que llega a escucharos.

COLOMBINA.—Permitid; pero antes de la fiesta preparada para esta noche he de hablar con el señor Arlequín y . . .

CRISPÍN.—No es preciso. A eso vine, enviado de su parte y de parte de mi señor, que os besa las manos.

COLOMBINA.—¿Y quién es vuestro señor, si puede saberse?

CRISPÍN.—El más noble caballero, el más poderoso . . . Permitid que por ahora calle su nombre; pronto habréis de conocerle. Mi señor desea saludar a doña Sirena y asistir a su fiesta esta noche.

COLOMBINA.—¡La fiesta! ¿No sabéis . . .?

CRISPÍN.—Lo sé. Mi deber es averiguarlo todo. Sé que hubo inconvenientes que pudieron estorbarla; pero no habrá ninguno, todo está prevenido.

COLOMBINA.—¿Cómo sabéis . . .?

CRISPÍN.—Yo os aseguro que no faltará nada. Suntuoso agasajo, luminarias y fuegos de artificio, músicos y cantores. Será la más lucida fiesta del mundo . . .

COLOMBINA.—¿Sois algún encantador, por ventura?

CRISPÍN.—Ya me iréis conociendo. Sólo os diré que por algo juntó hoy el destino a gente de tan buen entendimiento, incapaz de malograrlo con vanos escrúpulos. Mi señor sabe que esta noche asistirá a la fiesta el señor Polichinela, con su hija única, la hermosa Silvia, el mejor partido de esta ciudad. Mi señor ha de enamorarla, mi señor ha de casarse con ella y mi señor sabrá pagar como corresponde los buenos oficios de doña Sirena y los vuestros también si os prestáis a favorecerle.

COLOMBINA.—No andáis con rodeos. Debiera ofenderme vuestro atrevimiento.

CRISPÍN.—El tiempo apremia y no me dió lugar a ser comedido.

COLOMBINA.—Si ha de juzgarse del amo por el criado . . .

CRISPÍN.—No temáis. A mi amo le hallaréis el más cortés y atento caballero. Mi desvergüenza le permite a él mostrarse vergonzoso. Duras necesidades de la vida pueden obligar al más noble caballero

because to spare a woman's heart is no more foolishly presumptuous than to spare a man's life.[9]

CRISPIN: Now I realize that you aren't as dangerous to a man's eyes as you are to his ears.

COLUMBINE: Excuse me, but before the party that's been arranged for tonight I must speak with Mr. Harlequin and . . .

CRISPIN: That's not necessary. I've come for that purpose, having been sent by him and by my master, who kisses your hands.

COLUMBINE: And who is your master, if I may ask?

CRISPIN: The most noble gentleman and the most powerful. . . . Permit me to withhold his name for the moment; you will soon get to meet him. My master wishes to meet Madam Sirena and attend her party tonight.

COLUMBINE: Her party! Don't you know—?

CRISPIN: I know. My duty is to find out everything. I know that there were contretemps that threatened to prevent it; but there won't be any obstacles; everything has been taken care of.

COLUMBINE: How do you know—?

CRISPIN: I assure you that nothing will be lacking. Sumptuous food and drink, lanterns and fireworks, musicians and singers. It will be the most brilliant party in the world. . . .

COLUMBINE: Are you some magician, by chance?

CRISPIN: You'll soon get to know me. I'll merely say that it was not for nothing that destiny brought together today people of such great good sense, and most unlikely to throw away that sense on vain scruples. My master knows that the party tonight will be attended by Mr. Punchinello, with his only daughter, the lovely Sylvia, the best match in this city. My master will win her heart, my master will marry her, and my master is one who'll recompense duly the good offices of Madam Sirena, and yours as well, if you consent to assist him.

COLUMBINE: You don't beat around the bush. Your boldness ought to offend me.

CRISPIN: Matters are urgent and don't allow me to be polite.

COLUMBINE: If one is to judge the master by his servant . . .

CRISPIN: Have no fear. You'll find my master the most courteous and attentive gentleman. My effrontery allows him to appear bashful. The hard necessities of life may force the most noble gentleman to act like a

9. Presumably, Crispin is "sparing Columbine's heart" by assuring her that he isn't seriously seeking her love. This difficult sentence, with its precious conceit, was translated by Underhill as: "It is as foolish to trust a man while he lives as a woman while she loves." A neater epigram—but correct? Another remote possibility is: "because it is as foolish a conceit for men to spare lives as for women (to spare) hearts."

a empleos de rufián, como a la más noble dama a bajos oficios, y esta mezcla de ruindad y nobleza en un mismo sujeto desluce con el mundo. Habilidad es mostrar separado en dos sujetos lo que suele andar junto en uno solo. Mi señor y yo, con ser uno mismo, somos cada uno una parte del otro. ¡Si así fuera siempre! Todos llevamos en nosotros un gran señor de altivos pensamientos, capaz de todo lo grande y de todo lo bello . . . Y a su lado, el servidor humilde, el de las ruines obras, el que ha de emplearse en las bajas acciones a que obliga la vida . . . Todo el arte está en separarlos de tal modo, que cuando caemos en alguna bajeza podamos decir siempre: no fué mía, no fuí yo, fué mi criado. En la mayor miseria de nuestra vida siempre hay algo en nosotros que quiere sentirse superior a nosotros mismos. Nos despreciaríamos demasiado si no creyésemos valer más que nuestra vida . . . Ya sabéis quién es mi señor: el de los altivos pensamientos, el de los bellos sueños. Ya sabéis quién soy yo: el de los ruines empleos, el que siempre, muy bajo, rastrea y socava entre toda mentira y toda indignidad y toda miseria. Sólo hay algo en mí que me redime y me eleva a mis propios ojos. Esta lealtad de mi servidumbre, esta lealtad que se humilla y se arrastra para que otro pueda volar y pueda ser siempre el señor de los altivos pensamientos, el de los bellos sueños. (*Se oye música dentro.*)

COLOMBINA.—¿Qué música es ésa?

CRISPÍN.—La que mi señor trae a la fiesta, con todos sus pajes y todos sus criados y toda una corte de poetas y cantores presididos por el señor Arlequín, y toda una legión de soldados, con el Capitán al frente, escoltándole con antorchas . . .

COLOMBINA.—¿Quién es vuestro señor, que tanto puede? Corro a prevenir a mi señora . . .

CRISPÍN.—No es preciso. Ella acude.

Escena III

DICHOS *y* DOÑA SIRENA, *que sale por el pabellón*

SIRENA.—¿Qué es esto? ¿Quién previno esa música? ¿Qué tropel de gente llega a nuestra puerta?

COLOMBINA.—No preguntéis nada. Sabed que hoy llegó a esta ciudad un gran señor, y es él quien os ofrece la fiesta esta noche. Su criado os informará de todo. Yo aun no sabré deciros si hablé con un gran

pander, just as they may compel the noblest lady into shady dealings; and that combination of vileness and nobility in one and the same person discredits him in society. It's a shrewd ploy to exhibit separately in two persons the traits that are usually mingled in a single one. My master and I, though we are but one, are each a part of the other. If only things could always be that way! We all bear within us a great lord of exalted sentiments, capable of all that's great and beautiful. . . . And alongside him, the humble servant, the one of vile actions, the one who must undertake the low deeds which life forces on us. . . . The whole art consists in separating them in such a way that, when we become guilty of some unworthy deed, we can always say: "I'm not to blame; I didn't do it, my servant did." Amid the greatest wretchedness of our life there's always something in us that wants to feel superior to ourselves. We'd think too little of ourselves unless we believed we were of greater worth than our actual life. . . . Now you know who my master is: the man of exalted sentiments, the man of beautiful dreams. Now you know who I am: the man of vile tasks, the man at the bottom who hugs the ground and undermines it amid every lie, every baseness, and every unworthy action. Only, there's something in me that redeems me and elevates me in my own eyes: this loyalty of my servitude, this loyalty which degrades itself and crawls in order that another man may fly and always be the master with exalted sentiments, the man of beautiful dreams. (*Music is heard within.*)

COLUMBINE: What's that music?

CRISPIN: The music my master has brought to the party, with all his pages and all his servants and an entire royal court of poets and singers presided over by Mr. Harlequin, and an entire legion of soldiers with the Captain at their head, escorting him with torches. . . .

COLUMBINE: Who is your master, to have such power? I'm running off to inform my mistress. . . .

CRISPIN: No need for that. Here she comes.

Scene III

The above and MADAM SIRENA, *who enters by way of the pavilion.*

SIRENA: What's all this? Who arranged for this music? What's this troop of people arriving at our door?

COLUMBINE: Ask no questions. Let me tell you: a great lord arrived in this city today, and it's he who's offering you the party tonight. His servant will give you all the information. And I'm not even able to tell

loco o con un gran bribón. De cualquier modo, os aseguro que él es un hombre extraordinario . . .

SIRENA.—¿Luego no fué Arlequín?

COLOMBINA.—No preguntéis . . . Todo es como cosa de magia . . .

CRISPÍN.—Doña Sirena, mi señor os pide licencia para besaros las manos. Tan alta señora y tan noble señor no han de entender en intrigas impropias de su condición. Por eso, antes que él llegue a saludaros, yo he de decirlo todo. Yo sé de vuestra historia mil notables sucesos que, referidos, me asegurarían toda vuestra confianza . . . Pero fuera impertinencia puntualizarlos. Mi amo os asegura aquí (*Entregándole un papel*) con su firma la obligación que ha de cumpliros si de vuestra parte sabéis cumplir lo que aquí os propone.

SIRENA.—¿Qué papel y qué obligación es ésta? . . . (*Leyendo el papel para sí.*) ¡Cómo! ¿Cien mil escudos de presente y otros tantos a la muerte del señor Polichinela si llega a casarse con su hija? ¿Qué insolencia es ésta? ¿A una dama? ¿Sabéis con quién habláis? ¿Sabéis qué casa es ésta?

CRISPÍN.—Doña Sirena . . . , ¡excusad la indignación! No hay nadie presente que pueda importaros. Guardad ese papel junto con otros . . . , y no se hable más del asunto. Mi señor no os propone nada indecoroso, ni vos consintiríais en ello . . . Cuanto aquí sucede será obra de la casualidad y del amor. Fuí yo, el criado, el único que tramó estas cosas indignas. Vos sois siempre la noble dama, mi amo el noble señor, que al encontraros esta noche en la fiesta, hablaréis de mil cosas galantes y delicadas, mientras vuestros convidados pasean y conversan a vuestro alrededor, con admiraciones a la hermosura de las damas, al arte de sus galas, a la esplendidez del agasajo, a la dulzura de la música y a la gracia de los bailarines . . . ¿Y quién se atreverá a decir que no es esto todo? ¿No es así la vida, una fiesta en que la música sirve para disimular palabras y las palabras para disimular pensamientos? Que la música suene incesante, que la conversación se anime con alegres risas, que la cena esté bien servida . . . , es todo lo que importa a los convidados. Y ved aquí a mi señor, que llega a saludaros con toda gentileza.

you whether I've been speaking with a real lunatic or a real crook. At any rate, I assure you that he's an extraordinary man. . . .

SIRENA: Then, it wasn't Harlequin?

COLUMBINE: Don't ask. . . . It's all like a magic spell. . . .

CRISPIN: Madam Sirena, my master begs leave to kiss your hands. So lofty a lady and so noble a lord should have no part in intrigues unbefitting to their status. And so, before he comes to greet you, I must tell you everything. I know of a thousand remarkable events in your past life which, if I narrated them, would assure me of your full confidence. . . . But it would be impertinent to go into details. My master here assures you (*handing her a paper*) with his signature of the obligation he will be under toward you if on your part you can bring about what he here proposes.

SIRENA: What's this paper, and what's this obligation? (*Reading the paper to herself:*) What? A hundred thousand crowns right away, and the same amount upon the death of Mr. Punchinello, if your master manages to marry his daughter? What is this insolence? Such a proposition to a lady? Do you know who you're talking to? Do you know what house you're in?

CRISPIN: Madam Sirena, . . . spare me your indignation! There's no body present you have to watch out for. Keep this paper along with all the rest . . . and let's not discuss the matter further. My master isn't proposing anything unseemly to you, nor would you agree to anything like that. . . . Everything that happens here will be the result of chance and of love. I, the servant, was the only one who plotted these unworthy things. You remain always the noble lady; my master, the noble lord; and when you meet at the party tonight, you'll speak of a thousand gallant and delicate things, while your guests stroll and chat all around you, admiring the beauty of the ladies, the artistic nature of their finery, the splendidness of the food and drink, the sweetness of the music, and the gracefulness of the dancers. . . . And who will be so bold as to say there's any more to it? Isn't life like that?—a party at which the music is there to drown out the words, and the words are there to conceal the thoughts. Let the music play uninterruptedly, let the conversation grow lively with merry laughter, let the dinner be well served—that's all that matters to the guests. And now here's my master, coming to greet you with perfect gentility.

Escena IV

DICHOS, LEANDRO, ARLEQUÍN *y el* CAPITÁN, *que salen por la segunda derecha*

LEANDRO.—Doña Sirena, bésoos las manos.

SIRENA.—Caballero . . .

LEANDRO.—Mi criado os habrá dicho en mi nombre cuanto yo pudiera deciros.

CRISPÍN.—Mi señor, como persona grave, es de pocas palabras. Su admiración es muda.

ARLEQUÍN.—Pero sabe admirar sabiamente.

CAPITÁN.—El verdadero mérito.

ARLEQUÍN.—El verdadero valor.

CAPITÁN.—El arte incomparable de la poesía.

ARLEQUÍN.—La noble ciencia militar.

CAPITÁN.—En todo muestra su grandeza.

ARLEQUÍN.—Es el más noble caballero del mundo.

CAPITÁN.—Mi espada siempre estará a su servicio.

ARLEQUÍN.—He de consagrar a su gloria mi mejor poema.

CRISPÍN.—Basta, basta, que ofenderéis su natural modestia. Vedle, cómo quisiera ocultarse y desaparecer. Es una violeta.

SIRENA.—No necesita hablar quien de este modo hace hablar a todos en su alabanza. (*Después de un saludo y reverencia se van todos por la primera derecha.* A COLOMBINA.) ¿Qué piensas de todo esto, Colombina?

COLOMBINA.—Que el caballero tiene muy gentil figura y el criado muy gentil desvergüenza.

SIRENA.—Todo puede aprovecharse. Y yo no sé nada del mundo ni de los hombres, o la fortuna se entró hoy por mis puertas.

COLOMBINA.—Pues segura es entonces la fortuna; porque del mundo sabéis algo, y de los hombres, ¡no se diga!

SIRENA.—Risela y Laura, que son las primeras en llegar . . .

COLOMBINA.—¿Cuándo fueron ellas las últimas en llegar a una fiesta? Os dejo en su compañía, que yo no quiero perder de vista a nuestro caballero . . . (*Vase por la primera derecha.*)

Scene IV

The above, LEANDER, HARLEQUIN, *and the* CAPTAIN *enter from the second wing-space, right.*

LEANDER: Madam Sirena, I kiss your hands.

SIRENA: Sir . . .

LEANDER: My servant must surely have said on my behalf all that I could say to you.

CRISPIN: My master, being a serious person, is a man of few words. His is a mute admiration.

HARLEQUIN: But he knows how to admire wisely.

CAPTAIN: To admire true merit!

HARLEQUIN: To admire true valor!

CAPTAIN: The incomparable art of poetry!

HARLEQUIN: The noble military science!

CAPTAIN: He shows his greatness in everything he does.

HARLEQUIN: He's the most noble gentleman in the world.

CAPTAIN: My sword will always be at his disposal.

HARLEQUIN: I shall devote my finest poem to his honor.

CRISPIN: Enough, enough, or you'll wound his inborn modesty. Look at him, as if he were trying to hide and disappear! He's a shrinking violet.

SIRENA: A man doesn't need to speak when he can make everyone speak in his praise this way. (*After bows and curtseys, all the men exit into the first wing-space, right. To* COLUMBINE:) What do you think of all this, Columbine?

COLUMBINE: That the gentleman cuts a very genteel figure, and his servant possesses very genteel effrontery.

SIRENA: All of that can come in handy. And, unless I know nothing about society or men, good luck has walked into my door today.

COLUMBINE: Then, our good luck is a certainty, because you do know something about society, and as for men—what can I say!

SIRENA: Risela and Laura, who are the first to arrive . . .

COLUMBINE: When were those two ever the last to arrive at a party? I leave you in their company, because I don't want to let our gentleman out of my sight. . . . (*She exits into the first wing-space, right.*)

Escena V

DOÑA SIRENA, LAURA *y* RISELA, *que salen por la segunda derecha*

SIRENA.—¡Amigas! Ya comenzaba a dolerme de vuestra ausencia.

LAURA.—Pues, ¿es tan tarde?

SIRENA.—Siempre lo es para veros.

RISELA.—Otras dos fiestas dejamos por no faltar a vuestra casa.

LAURA.—Por más que alguien nos dijo que no sería esta noche por hallaros algo indispuesta.

SIRENA.—Sólo por dejar mal a los maldicientes, aun muriendo la hubiera tenido.

RISELA.—Y nosotras nos hubiéramos muerto y no hubiéramos dejado de asistir a ella.

LAURA.—¿No sabéis la novedad?

RISELA.—No se habla de otra cosa.

LAURA.—Dicen que ha llegado un personaje misterioso. Unos dicen que es embajador secreto de Venecia o de Francia.

RISELA.—Otros dicen que viene a buscar esposa para el Gran Turco.

LAURA.—Aseguran que es lindo como un Adonis.

RISELA.—Si nos fuera posible conocerle . . . Debisteis invitarle a vuestra fiesta.

SIRENA.—No fué preciso, amigas, que él mismo envió un embajador a pedir licencia para ser recibido. Y en mi casa está y le veréis muy pronto.

LAURA.—¿Qué decís? Ved si anduvimos acertadas en dejarlo todo por asistir a vuestra casa.

SIRENA.—¡Cuántas nos envidiarán esta noche!

LAURA.—Todos rabian por conocerle.

SIRENA.—Pues yo nada hice por lograrlo. Bastó que él supiera que yo tenía fiesta en mi casa.

RISELA.—Siempre fué lo mismo con vos. No llega persona importante a la ciudad que luego no os ofrezca sus respetos.

LAURA.—Ya se me tarda en verle . . . Llevadnos a su presencia, por vuestra vida.

RISELA.—Sí, sí, llevadnos.

SIRENA.—Permitid, que llega el señor Polichinela con su familia . . . Pero id sin mí; no os será difícil hallarle.

RISELA.—Sí, sí; vamos, Laura.

LAURA.—Vamos, Risela. Antes de que aumente la confusión y no nos sea posible acercarnos. (*Vanse por la primera derecha.*)

Scene V

MADAM SIRENA, LAURA, *and* RISELA, *the last two entering from the second wing-space, right.*

SIRENA: My friends! I was beginning to grieve over your absence.

LAURA: Is it so late, then?

SIRENA: It always seems late when I'm waiting to see *you*.

RISELA: We passed up two other parties in order to be sure to come here.

LAURA: Especially since somebody told us that yours wouldn't take place tonight because you were feeling a little indisposed.

SIRENA: If only to show up those slanderers, I would have given the party even if I were dying.

RISELA: And even if we had died, *we* wouldn't have failed to attend it.

LAURA: Don't you know the news?

RISELA: No one's talking about anything else.

LAURA: They say that a mysterious character has come to town. Some say he's a secret ambassador from Venice or France.

RISELA: Others say he's come to find a bride for the sultan of Turkey.

LAURA: They assure us he's as handsome as Adonis.

RISELA: If we could possibly meet him . . . You must have invited him to your party.

SIRENA: That wasn't necessary, my friends, because he himself sent an ambassador to beg leave to be admitted. And he's in my house and you'll see him very soon.

LAURA: What's that you say? See how right we were to pass up everything else and come to your house!

SIRENA: All the women who'll envy us tonight!

LAURA: Everyone's dying to meet him.

SIRENA: Well, I did nothing to get hold of him. All it took was for him to hear I was giving a party at my house.

RISELA: It's always been the same with you. No important person arrives in town without paying you his respects immediately.

LAURA: I can't wait to see him. . . . Take us where he is, I implore you!

RISELA: Yes, yes, take us!

SIRENA: Excuse me, because Mr. Punchinello and his family are arriving. . . . But go without me; you'll have no trouble finding him.

RISELA: Yes, yes; let's go, Laura!

LAURA: Let's go, Risela! Before the crowd grows and we can't get near him! (*They exit into the first wing-space, right.*)

Escena VI

DOÑA SIRENA, POLICHINELA, *la* SEÑORA DE POLICHINELA *y* SILVIA, *que salen por la segunda derecha*

SIRENA.—¡Oh señor Polichinela! Ya temí que no vendríais. Hasta ahora no comenzó para mí la fiesta.

POLICHINELA.—No fué culpa mía la tardanza. Fué de mi mujer, que entre cuarenta vestidos no supo nunca cuál ponerse.

SEÑORA DE POLICHINELA.—Si por él fuera, me presentaría de cualquier modo . . . Ved cómo vengo de sofocada por apresurarme.

SIRENA.—Venís hermosa como nunca.

POLICHINELA.—Pues aún no trae la mitad de sus joyas. No podría con tanto peso.

SIRENA.—¿Y quién mejor puede ufanarse con que su esposa ostente el fruto de una riqueza adquirida con vuestro trabajo?

SEÑORA DE POLICHINELA.—Pero ¿no es hora ya de disfrutar de ella, como yo le digo, y de tener más nobles aspiraciones? Figuraos que ahora quiere casar a nuestra hija con un negociante.

SIRENA.—¡Oh señor Polichinela! Vuestra hija merece mucho más que un negociante. No hay que pensar en eso. No debéis sacrificar su corazón por ningún interés. ¿Qué dices tú, Silvia?

POLICHINELA.—Ella preferiría algún barbilindo, que, muy a pesar mío, es muy dada a novelas y poesías.

SILVIA.—Yo haré siempre lo que mi padre ordene si a mi madre no le contraría y a mí no me disgusta.

SIRENA.—Eso es hablar con juicio.

SEÑORA DE POLICHINELA.—Tu padre piensa que sólo el dinero vale y se estima en el mundo.

POLICHINELA.—Yo pienso que sin dinero no hay cosa que valga ni se estime en el mundo; que es el precio de todo.

SIRENA.—¡No habléis así! ¿Y las virtudes, y el saber, y la nobleza?

POLICHINELA.—Todo tiene su precio, ¿quién lo duda? Nadie mejor que yo lo sabe, que compré mucho de todo eso, y no muy caro.

SIRENA.—¡Oh señor Polichinela! Es humorada vuestra. Bien sabéis que el dinero no es todo, y que si vuestra hija se enamora de algún noble caballero, no sería bien contrariarla. Yo sé que tenéis un sensible corazón de padre.

POLICHINELA.—Eso sí. Por mi hija sería yo capaz de todo.

SIRENA.—¿Hasta de arruinaros?

Scene VI

MADAM SIRENA, PUNCHINELLO, PUNCHINELLO'S WIFE, *and* SYLVIA, *the last three entering from the second wing-space, right.*

SIRENA: Oh, Mr. Punchinello! I was beginning to fear that you wouldn't come. For me, the party has only begun right now.

PUNCHINELLO: I'm not to blame for the delay. The one at fault is my wife, who, with forty dresses, can never choose which one to wear.

PUNCHINELLO'S WIFE: If it were up to him, I'd show myself in public any which way. . . . Look how out of breath I am from rushing.

SIRENA: You look more beautiful than ever.

PUNCHINELLO: And she's not even wearing half of her jewelry. She couldn't wear it all, it weighs so much.

SIRENA: And who, better than you, may take pride in your wife's displaying the fruits of a wealth acquired through your labors?

PUNCHINELLO'S WIFE: But isn't it high time to enjoy that wealth, as I keep telling him, and to have more noble aspirations? Just imagine: he now wants our daughter to marry a businessman.

SIRENA: Oh, Mr. Punchinello! Your daughter deserves much more than a businessman. You shouldn't even think about it. You mustn't sacrifice her heart to any self-interest. What do you say, Sylvia?

PUNCHINELLO: She'd prefer some young whippersnapper, because, to my great regret, she's very fond of novels and poetry.

SYLVIA: I'll always do what my father orders, if my mother isn't opposed to it and it doesn't displease me.

SIRENA: That's a sensible attitude.

PUNCHINELLO'S WIFE: Your father thinks that only money counts and is esteemed in society.

PUNCHINELLO: I think that, without money, nothing counts or is esteemed in society, because money is the price of everything.

SIRENA: Don't talk that way! What about the virtues, knowledge, and nobility?

PUNCHINELLO: They all have their price, who can doubt it? No one knows that better than I do, because I've bought a lot of all that, and not too dearly.

SIRENA: Oh, Mr. Punchinello! That's a caprice of yours. You're well aware that money isn't everything, and that if your daughter falls in love with some noble gentleman, it wouldn't be right to oppose her. I know you have a tender father's heart.

PUNCHINELLO: That I do. For my daughter I'd be capable of anything.

SIRENA: Even of ruining yourself financially?

POLICHINELA.—Eso no sería una prueba de cariño. Antes sería capaz de robar, de asesinar . . . de todo.

SIRENA.—Ya sé que siempre sabríais rehacer vuestra fortuna. Pero la fiesta se anima. Ven conmigo, Silvia. Para danzar téngote destinado un caballero, que habéis de ser la más lucida pareja . . . (*Se dirigen todos a la primera derecha. Al ir a salir el señor* POLICHINELA, CRISPÍN, *que entra por la segunda derecha, le detiene.*)

Escena VII

CRISPÍN *y* POLICHINELA

CRISPÍN.—¡Señor Polichinela! Con licencia.

POLICHINELA.—¿Quién me llama? ¿Qué me queréis?

CRISPÍN.—¿No recordáis de mí? No es extraño. El tiempo todo lo borra, y cuando es algo enojoso lo borrado, no deja ni siquiera el borrón como recuerdo, sino que se apresura a pintar sobre él con alegres colores, esos alegres colores con que ocultáis al mundo vuestras jorobas. Señor Polichinela, cuando yo os conocí apenas las cubrían unos descoloridos andrajos.

POLICHINELA.—¿Y quién eres tú y dónde pudiste conocerme?

CRISPÍN.—Yo era un mozuelo, tu eras ya todo un hombre. Pero ¿has olvidado ya tantas gloriosas hazañas por esos mares, tantas victorias ganadas al turco, a que no poco contribuímos con nuestro heroico esfuerzo, unidos los dos al mismo noble remo en la misma gloriosa nave?

POLICHINELA.—¡Imprudente! ¡Calla o . . . !

CRISPÍN.—O harás conmigo como con tu primer amo en Nápoles, y con tu primera mujer en Bolonia, y con aquel mercader judío en Venecia . . .

POLICHINELA.—¡Calla! ¿Quién eres tú, que tanto sabes y tanto hablas?

CRISPÍN.—Soy . . . , lo que fuiste. Y quien llegará a ser lo que eres . . . , como tú llegaste. No con tanta violencia como tú, porque los tiempos son otros y ya sólo asesinan los locos y los enamorados y cuatro pobretes que aún asaltan a mano armada al transeúnte por calles oscuras o caminos solitarios. ¡Carne de horca, despreciable!

PUNCHINELLO: That wouldn't be a proof of affection. Rather, I'd be capable of robbing, murdering, . . . anything.

SIRENA: I know that you'd always be able to put together another fortune. But the party is getting lively. Come with me, Sylvia. As a dancing partner I have in mind for you such a fine gentleman that you'll be the most brilliant couple on the floor. . . . (*They all head for the first wing-space, right. As* MR. PUNCHINELLO *is about to exit,* CRISPIN, *who enters from the second wing-space, right, detains him.*)

Scene VII

CRISPIN *and* PUNCHINELLO.

CRISPIN: Mr. Punchinello! By your leave.

PUNCHINELLO: Who's calling me? What do you want of me?

CRISPIN: You don't remember me? That's not strange. Time blots out everything, and when it's something vexing that has been blotted out, it leaves not even the blot as a memento, but hastens to paint it over with cheerful colors, those cheerful colors with which you conceal your humps from the world.[10] Mr. Punchinello, when I first met you, they were barely covered up with a few faded tatters.

PUNCHINELLO: And who are you and where could you have met me?

CRISPIN: I was a youngster, and you were already a grown man. But have you forgotten all those glorious exploits on the sea, all those victories over the Turks, to which we made no small contribution with our heroic efforts, both of us chained to the same noble oar in the same glorious ship?

PUNCHINELLO: Indiscreet fellow! Be quiet, or—!

CRISPIN: Or you'll do the same to me as to your first master in Naples, and to your first wife in Bologna, and to that Jewish merchant in Venice. . . .

PUNCHINELLO: Quiet! Who are you, to know so much and talk so much?

CRISPIN: I am . . . what you once were. And the man who'll get to be what you now are . . . the same way you got there. But not as violently as you, because these are different times, and the only killers now are madmen and lovers and a handful of poor souls who still use weapons to attack passersby on dark streets or lonely roads. Contemptible gallows-bait!

---

10. The humps on Punchinello's back and chest are probably only metaphorical here, but they allude to the traditional appearance of Punchinello in Italian Comedy.

POLICHINELA.—¿Y qué quieres de mí? Dinero, ¿no es eso? Ya nos veremos más despacio. No es éste el lugar . . .

CRISPÍN.—No tiembles por tu dinero. Sólo deseo ser tu amigo, tu aliado, como en aquellos tiempos.

POLICHINELA.—¿Qué puedo hacer por ti?

CRISPÍN.—No; ahora soy yo quien va a servirte, quien quiere obligarte con una advertencia . . . (*Haciéndole que mire a la primera derecha.*) ¿Ves allí a tu hija cómo danza con un joven caballero y cómo sonríe ruborosa al oír sus galanterías? Ese caballero es mi amo.

POLICHINELA.—¿Tu amo? Será entonces un aventurero, un hombre de fortuna, un bandido como . . .

CRISPÍN.—¿Como nosotros . . . , vas a decir? No; es más peligroso que nosotros, porque, como ves, su figura es bella, y hay en su mirada un misterio de encanto, y en su voz una dulzura que llega al corazón y le conmueve como si contara una historia triste. ¿No es esto bastante para enamorar a cualquier mujer? No dirás que no te he advertido. Corre y separa a tu hija de ese hombre, y no le permitas que baile con él ni que vuelva a escucharle en su vida.

POLICHINELA.—¿Y dices que es tu amo y así le sirves?

CRISPÍN.—¿Lo extrañas? ¿Te olvidas ya de cuando fuiste criado? Yo aún no pienso asesinarle.

POLICHINELA.—Dices bien; un amo es siempre odioso. Y en servirme a mí, ¿qué interés es el tuyo?

CRISPÍN.—Llegar a buen puerto, como llegamos tantas veces remando juntos. Entonces, tú me decías alguna vez: "Tú, que eres fuerte, rema por mí . . ." En esta galera de ahora eres tú más fuerte que yo; rema por mí, por el fiel amigo de entonces, que la vida es muy pesada galera y yo llevo remado mucho. (*Vase por la segunda derecha.*)

Escena VIII

El SEÑOR POLICHINELA, DOÑA SIRENA, *la* SEÑORA DE POLICHINELA, RISELA *y* LAURA, *que salen por la primera derecha*

LAURA.—Sólo doña Sirena sabe ofrecer fiestas semejantes.

RISELA.—Y la de esta noche excedió a todas.

SIRENA.—La presencia de tan singular caballero fué un nuevo atractivo.

PUNCHINELLO: And what do you want of me? Money, right? We'll see each other at another time. This isn't the place for it. . . .

CRISPIN: Don't tremble for your money. All I want is to be your friend, your ally, as in the old days.

PUNCHINELLO: What can I do for you?

CRISPIN: No; today I'm the one who's going to serve *you*, who wants to oblige you with a warning. . . . (*Directing* PUNCHINELLO*'s gaze toward the first wing-space, right:*) Do you see your daughter dancing there with a young gentleman, smiling and blushing as she listens to his sweet talk? That gentleman is my master.

PUNCHINELLO: Your master? Then he must be an adventurer, a sharpster, a bandit like . . .

CRISPIN: Like you and me, you were going to say? No; he's more dangerous than we are, because as you see, he's good-looking, and his eyes possess a mystery of enchantment, and his voice has a sweetness that touches the heart and moves it as if he were telling a sad story. Isn't that enough to make any woman fall in love? Don't say I haven't warned you. Run and take your daughter away from that man, and don't let her dance with him or listen to him again as long as she lives!

PUNCHINELLO: You say he's your master, and you serve him in this manner?

CRISPIN: You find it peculiar? Have you already forgotten the days when you were a servant? At least I don't intend to murder him.

PUNCHINELLO: You're right; a master is always hateful. But what gain do you expect from doing a favor to me?

CRISPIN: To reach a snug harbor, just as we did so often when we were rowing together. In those days you sometimes said to me: "You're the strong one, row for me." . . . In the galley we're now in, you're stronger than I am; row for me, for the faithful friend of the past, because life is a very heavy galley and I've done a lot of rowing. (*He exits into the second wing space, right.*)

Scene VIII

PUNCHINELLO, MADAM SIRENA, PUNCHINELLO'S WIFE, RISELA, *and* LAURA, *all the women entering from the first wing-space, right.*

LAURA: Only Madam Sirena knows how to give parties like this one.

RISELA: And tonight's has outdone all the rest.

SIRENA: The presence of such an eminent gentleman was a new attraction.

POLICHINELA.—¿Y Silvia? ¿Dónde quedó Silvia? ¿Cómo dejaste a nuestra hija?

SIRENA.—Callad, señor Polichinela, que vuestra hija se halla en excelente compañía, y en mi casa siempre está segura.

RISELA.—No hubo atenciones más que para ella.

LAURA.—Para ella es todo el agrado.

RISELA.—Y todos los suspiros.

POLICHINELA.—¿De quién? ¿De ese caballero misterioso? Pues no me contenta. Y ahora mismo . . .

SIRENA.—¡Pero, señor Polichinela! . . .

POLICHINELA.—¡Dejadme, dejadme! Yo sé lo que me hago. (*Vase por la primera derecha.*)

SIRENA.—¿Qué le ocurre? ¿Qué destemplanza es ésta?

SEÑORA DE POLICHINELA.—¿Veis qué hombre? ¡Capaz será de una grosería con el caballero! ¿Que ha de casar a su hija con algún mercader u hombre de baja estofa! ¡Que ha de hacerla desgraciada para toda la vida!

SIRENA.—¡Eso no! . . . , que sois su madre y algo ha de valer vuestra autoridad . . .

SEÑORA DE POLICHINELA.—¡Ved! Sin duda dijo alguna impertinencia, y el caballero ya deja la mano de Silvia y se retira cabizbajo.

LAURA.—Y el señor Polichinela parece reprender a vuestra hija . . .

SIRENA.—¡Vamos, vamos! Que no puede consentirse tanta tiranía.

RISELA.—Ahora vemos, señora Polichinela, que con todas vuestras riquezas no sois menos desgraciada.

SEÑORA DE POLICHINELA.—No lo sabéis, que algunas veces llegó hasta golpearme.

LAURA.—¿Qué decís? ¿Y fuisteis mujer para consentirlo?

SEÑORA DE POLICHINELA.—Luego cree componerlo con traerme algún regalo.

SIRENA.—¡Menos mal! Que hay maridos que no lo componen con nada. (*Vanse todas por la primera derecha.*)

Escena IX

LEANDRO *y* CRISPÍN, *que salen por la segunda derecha*

CRISPÍN.—¿Qué tristeza, qué abatimiento es ése? ¡Con mayor alegría pensé hallarte!

PUNCHINELLO: And Sylvia? Where is Sylvia? How was our daughter when you left her?

SIRENA: Be still, Mr. Punchinello; your daughter is in excellent company, and she's always safe in my house.

RISELA: He paid attention to nobody but her.

LAURA: His affability is entirely for her.

RISELA: And every sigh.

PUNCHINELLO: Whose? That mysterious gentleman's? Well, that doesn't please me. And this very moment . . .

SIRENA: But, Mr. Punchinello! . . .

PUNCHINELLO: Let me go, let me go! I know what I'm doing. (*He exits into the first wing-space, right.*)

SIRENA: What's wrong with him? Why is he so irritable?

PUNCHINELLO'S WIFE: See what kind of man he is? He'd even go so far as to be rude to the gentleman! He's got to marry off his daughter to some merchant or lower-class man! He's got to make her unhappy for her whole life!

SIRENA: Oh, no! . . . You're her mother, and you must have some say in the matter. . . .

PUNCHINELLO'S WIFE: Look! I'm sure he's said something uncalled-for, and now the gentleman is dropping Sylvia's hand and withdrawing in confusion.

LAURA: And Mr. Punchinello seems to be reprimanding your daughter. . . .

SIRENA: Let's go, let's go! Such tyranny is not to be tolerated.

RISELA: Now we see, Mrs. Punchinello, that with all your wealth you're still unhappy.

PUNCHINELLO'S WIFE: You don't know it all: sometimes he's even struck me.

LAURA: What's that you say? And you actually put up with that?

PUNCHINELLO'S WIFE: Afterwards he thinks he can make amends by bringing me some gift.

SIRENA: That's good, at least. There are husbands who don't make amends at all. (*They all exit into the first wing-space, right.*)

Scene IX

LEANDER *and* CRISPIN *enter from the second wing-space, right.*

CRISPIN: What's this sadness, this depression? I thought I'd find you happier than this!

LEANDRO.—Hasta ahora no me vi perdido; hasta ahora no me importó menos perderme. Huyamos, Crispín; huyamos de esta ciudad antes de que nadie pueda descubrirnos y vengan a saber lo que somos.

CRISPÍN.—Si huyéramos, es cuando todos lo sabrían y cuando muchos correrían hasta detenernos y hacernos volver a nuestro pesar, que no parece bien ausentarnos con tanta descortesía, sin despedirnos de gente tan atenta.

LEANDRO.—No te burles, Crispín, que estoy desesperado.

CRISPÍN.—¡Así eres! Cuando nuestras esperanzas llevan mejor camino.

LEANDRO.—¿Qué puedo esperar? Quisiste que fingiera un amor, y mal sabré fingirlo.

CRISPÍN.—¿Por qué?

LEANDRO.—Porque amo, amo con toda verdad y con toda mi alma.

CRISPÍN.—¿A Silvia? ¿Y de eso te lamentas?

LEANDRO.—¡Nunca pensé que pudiera amarse de este modo! ¡Nunca pensé que yo pudiera amar! En mi vida errante por todos los caminos, no fuí siquiera el que siempre pasa, sino el que siempre huye, enemiga la tierra, enemigos los hombres, enemiga la luz del sol. La fruta del camino, hurtada, no ofrecida, dejó acaso en mis labios algún sabor de amores, y alguna vez, después de muchos días azarosos, en el descanso de una noche, la serenidad del cielo me hizo soñar con algo que fuera en mi vida como aquel cielo de la noche que traía a mi alma el reposo de su serenidad. Y así esta noche, en el encanto de la fiesta . . . , me pareció que era un descanso en mi vida . . . , y soñaba . . . ¡He soñado! Pero mañana será otra vez la huída azarosa, será la justicia que nos persigue . . . , y no quiero que me halle aquí, donde está ella, donde ella puede avergonzarse de haberme visto.

CRISPÍN.—Yo creí ver que eras acogido con agrado . . . Y no fuí yo solo en advertirlo. Doña Sirena y nuestros buenos amigos el capitán y el poeta le hicieron de ti los mayores elogios. A su excelente madre, la señora Polichinela, que sólo sueña emparentar con un noble, le pareciste el yerno de sus ilusiones. En cuanto al señor Polichinela . . .

LEANDRO.—Sospecha de nosotros . . . Nos conoce . . .

CRISPÍN.—Sí; al señor Polichinela no es fácil engañarle como a un hombre vulgar. A un zorro viejo como él hay que engañarle con lealtad. Por eso me pareció mejor medio prevenirle de todo.

LEANDRO.—¿Cómo?

CRISPÍN.—Sí; él me conoce de antiguo . . . Al decirle que tú eres mi

LEANDER: Up to now I never considered myself a lost man; up to now it never mattered at all to me if I *was* lost. Let's run away, Crispin; let's flee from this city before anyone is able to find us out and learn what we are!

CRISPIN: If we ran away, that's when everyone would find out, and many would pursue us till they caught us and made us come back against our will; it doesn't seem advisable to take our leave so rudely, without saying good-bye to such considerate people.

LEANDER: Don't laugh at me, Crispin; I'm in despair.

CRISPIN: That's just like you! When our hopes are set on a surer path!

LEANDER: What can I hope for? You wanted me to pretend to be in love, and I won't be able to pretend.

CRISPIN: Why not?

LEANDER: Because I *am* in love, in love for real and with all my soul.

CRISPIN: With Sylvia? And you're complaining about that?

LEANDER: I never thought anyone could love this way! I never thought it could happen to me! During my wandering life on one road after another, I wasn't merely the eternal passerby, I was the eternal runaway! The earth was my enemy, people were my enemies, the sunlight was my enemy. Wayside fruits—stolen, not offered—perhaps left some taste of love on my lips, and at times, after many a difficult day, while reposing one night the clearness of the sky made me dream of something that might be in my life the equivalent of that night sky which bestowed the calmness of its clarity on my soul. And similarly tonight, in the enchantment of the party, . . . I felt that there was a repose in my life, . . . and I dreamed. . . . I've dreamed! But tomorrow we'll be back to our wearisome escape, and the police will be after us, . . . and I don't want them to find me here, where she is, where she may be ashamed of ever meeting me.

CRISPIN: I thought I saw you being welcomed affably. . . . And I wasn't the only one who observed it. Madam Sirena and our good friends, the captain and the poet, praised you to the skies. To her worthy mother, Mrs. Punchinello, who dreams of nothing but becoming related to a nobleman, you seemed like the son-in-law of her fondest hopes. As for Mr. Punchinello . . .

LEANDER: He suspects us. . . . He knows us. . . .

CRISPIN: Yes; it isn't easy to deceive Mr. Punchinello like an ordinary man. An old fox like him has to be deceived by an appearance of loyalty. That's why I thought the best approach was to inform him of everything.

LEANDER: What?

CRISPIN: Yes; he knows me from way back. . . . When I told him that

amo, supuso, con razón, que el amo sería digno del criado. Y yo, por corresponder a su confianza, le advertí que de ningún modo consintiera que hablaras con su hija.

LEANDRO.—¿Eso hiciste? ¿Y qué puedo esperar?

CRISPÍN.—¡Necio eres! Que el señor Polichinela ponga todo su empeño en que no vuelvas a ver a su hija.

LEANDRO.—¡No lo entiendo!

CRISPÍN.—Y que de este modo sea nuestro mejor aliado, porque bastará que él se oponga, para que su mujer le lleve la contraria y su hija se enamore de ti más locamente. Tú no sabes lo que es una joven, hija de un padre rico, criada en el mayor regalo, cuando ve por primera vez en su vida que algo se opone a su voluntad. Estoy seguro de que esta misma noche, antes de terminar la fiesta, consigue burlar la vigilancia de su padre para hablar todavía contigo.

LEANDRO.—Pero ¿no ves que nada me importa del señor Polichinela ni del mundo entero? Que es a ella, sólo a ella, a quien yo no quiero parecer indigno y despreciable . . . , a quien yo no quiero mentir.

CRISPÍN.—¡Bah! ¡Deja locuras! No es posible retroceder. Piensa en la suerte que nos espera si vacilamos en seguir adelante. ¿Que te has enamorado? Ese amor verdadero nos servirá mejor que si fuera fingido. Tal vez de otro modo hubieras querido ir demasiado de prisa; y si la osadía y la insolencia convienen para todo, sólo en amor sienta bien a los hombres algo de timidez. La timidez del hombre hace ser más atrevidas a las mujeres. Y si lo dudas, aquí tienes a la inocente Silvia, que llega con el mayor sigilo y sólo espera para acercarse a ti que yo me retire o me esconda.

LEANDRO.—¿Silvia dices?

CRISPÍN.—¡Chito! ¡Que pudiera espantarse! Y cuando esté a tu lado, mucha discreción . . . , pocas palabras, pocas . . . Adora, contempla, admira, y deja que hable por ti el encanto de esta noche azul, propicia a los amores, y esa música que apaga sus sones entre la arboleda y llega como triste de la alegría de la fiesta.

LEANDRO.—No te burles, Crispín; ni te burles de este amor que será mi muerte.

CRISPÍN.—¿Por qué he de burlarme? Yo sé bien que no conviene siempre rastrear. Alguna vez hay que volar por el cielo para mejor dominar la tierra. Vuela tú ahora; yo sigo arrastrándome. ¡El mundo será nuestro! (*Vase por la segunda izquierda.*)

you were my master, he assumed, rightly, that the master would be worthy of the servant. And I, to play up to his trust in me, warned him by all means not to allow you to talk to his daughter.

LEANDER: You did such a thing? And what can I expect now?

CRISPIN: You're a fool! You can expect that Mr. Punchinello will do his utmost to make sure you don't see his daughter again.

LEANDER: I don't understand!

CRISPIN: And that, by doing so, he'll become our best ally, because it will only take his opposition to make his wife adopt the contrary view and his daughter fall more madly in love with you. You don't know what a young woman is like—daughter of a wealthy father, raised in the lap of luxury—when, for the first time in her life, she meets some opposition to her own wishes. I'm sure that, this very night, before the party is over, she'll manage to elude her father's vigilance in order to go on speaking with you.

LEANDER: But can't you see that I don't care at all about Mr. Punchinello or the whole world? Because it's in her eyes, only hers, that I don't want to look unworthy and contemptible, . . . she's the only one I don't want to lie to.

CRISPIN: Bah! Stop that crazy talk! It's impossible to retreat. Think about the fate that awaits us if we hesitate to push forward. What if you've fallen in love? That genuine love will serve our turn better than if it were mere pretense. Maybe under other circumstances you'd have wanted to move too quickly; and though boldness and insolence are never out of place, it's only in matters of love that a little shyness is becoming to a man. A man's shyness makes the woman act more daringly. If you doubt that, here you have the innocent Sylvia, who has come here with the utmost caution and is only waiting for me to leave or hide before she approaches you.

LEANDER: You said Sylvia?

CRISPIN: Sh! She might get frightened away! And when she's with you, be very discreet . . . few words, very few. . . . Adore her, gaze at her, admire her, and let your spokesmen be the magic of this blue night, propitious to lovers, and that music whose tones are dying away in the grove and coming to us, as though they were sad, from the happiness of the party.

LEANDER: Don't make fun, Crispin; don't make fun of this love which will be the death of me.

CRISPIN: Why should I be making fun of you? I'm well aware that it isn't always appropriate to crawl on the ground. At times you have to fly through the sky in order to dominate the earth more effectively. Fly now; I'll go on hugging the ground. The world will be ours! (*He exits through the second wing-space, left.*)

Escena X

LEANDRO *y* SILVIA, *que sale por la primera derecha. Al final,* CRISPÍN

LEANDRO.—¡Silvia!
SILVIA.—¿Sois vos? Perdonad; no creí hallaros aquí.
LEANDRO.—Huí de la fiesta. Su alegría me entristece.
SILVIA.—¿También a vos?
LEANDRO.—¿También, decís? ¡También os entristece la alegría! . . .
SILVIA.—Mi padre se ha enojado conmigo. ¡Nunca me habló de este modo! Y con vos también estuvo desatento. ¿Le perdonáis?
LEANDRO.—Sí; lo perdono todo. Pero no le enojéis por mi causa. Volved a la fiesta, que han de buscaros, y si os hallaran aquí a mi lado . . .
SILVIA.—Tenéis razón. Pero volved vos también. ¿Porqué habéis de estar triste?
LEANDRO.—No; yo saldré sin que nadie lo advierta . . . Debo ir muy lejos.
SILVIA.—¿Qué decís? ¿No os trajeron asuntos de importancia a esta ciudad? ¿No debíais permanecer aquí mucho tiempo?
LEANDRO.—¡No, no! ¡Ni un día más! ¡Ni un día más!
SILVIA.—Entonces . . . ¿me habéis mentido?
LEANDRO.—¡Mentir! . . . No . . . No digáis que he mentido. No; ésta es la única verdad de mi vida . . . ¡Este sueño que no debe tener despertar! (*Se oye a lo lejos la música de una canción hasta que cae el telón.*)
SILVIA.—Es Arlequín que canta . . . ¿Qué os sucede? ¿Lloráis? ¿Es la música la que os hace llorar? ¿Por qué no decirme vuestra tristeza?
LEANDRO.—¿Mi tristeza? Ya la dice esa canción. Escuchadla.
SILVIA.—Desde aquí sólo la música se percibe; las palabras se pierden. ¿No la sabéis? Es una canción al silencio de la noche, y se llama *El reino de las almas.* ¿No la sabéis?
LEANDRO.—Decidla.
SILVIA:

La noche amorosa, sobre los amantes
tiende de su cielo el dosel nupcial.
La noche ha prendido sus claros diamantes
en el terciopelo de un cielo estival.

Scene X

LEANDER *and* SYLVIA, *who enters from the first wing-space, right. At the end of the scene,* CRISPIN.

LEANDER: Sylvia!

SYLVIA: It's you? Excuse me; I didn't think I'd find you here.

LEANDER: I ran away from the party. Its merriment makes me unhappy.

SYLVIA: You, too?

LEANDER: "You, too," you said? Happiness makes *you* sad, too?

SYLVIA: My father got angry with me. He's never spoken to me like that! And he was impolite to you, also. Can you forgive him?

LEANDER: Yes; I forgive everything. But don't get him angry on my account. Go back to the party, because they must be looking for you, and if they found you here with me . . .

SYLVIA: You're right. But you come back, too. Why should you be unhappy?

LEANDER: No; I'll leave without anyone noticing. . . . I must go very far away.

SYLVIA: What are you saying? Didn't affairs of importance bring you to this city? Didn't you need to stay here for a long time?

LEANDER: No, no! Not one day more! Not one day more!

SYLVIA: Then, . . . you lied to me?

LEANDER: Lied! . . . No. . . . Don't say I lied. No; this is the only true thing in my life. . . . This dream from which there ought to be no awakening! (*From the distance is heard the music of a song, until the curtain falls.*)

SYLVIA: It's Harlequin singing. . . . What's wrong with you? You're crying? Is it the music that makes you cry? Why don't you tell me why you're sad?

LEANDER: Why I'm sad? That song says it all. Listen to it.

SYLVIA: From here I can make out only the music; the words fade away. You don't know it? It's a song to the silence of the night, and it's called "The Realm of Souls." You don't know it?

LEANDER: Recite the words.

SYLVIA:[11]

The night loves lovers; gently over them
She spreads a nuptial canopy on high,
And vividly with many a shining gem
She studs the velvet of the summer sky.

---

11. A performing version in English verse is provided here. A more literal line-for-line translation will be found in the Appendix.

El jardín en sombra no tiene colores,
y es en el misterio de su oscuridad
susurro el follaje, aroma las flores,
y amor . . . un deseo dulce de llorar.
La voz que suspira, y la voz que canta
y la voz que dice palabras de amor,
impiedad parecen en la noche santa,
como una blasfemia entre una oración.
¡Alma del silencio, que yo reverencio,
tiene tu silencio la inefable voz
de los que murieron amando en silencio,
de los que callaron muriendo de amor,
de los que en la vida, por amarnos mucho,
tal vez no supieron su amor expresar!
¿No es la voz acaso que en la noche escucho
y cuando amor dice, dice eternidad?
¡Madre de mi alma! ¿No es luz de tus ojos
    la luz de esa estrella
que como una lágrima de amor infinito
    en la noche tiembla?
¡Dile a la que hoy amo que yo no amé nunca
    más que a ti en la tierra,
y desde que has muerto sólo me ha besado
    la luz de esa estrella!

LEANDRO:
¡Madre de mi alma! Yo no he amado nunca
    más que a ti en la tierra,
y desde que has muerto sólo me ha besado
    la luz de esa estrella.

(*Quedan en silencio, abrazados y mirándose.*)

CRISPÍN.—(*Que aparece por la segunda izquierda. Aparte.*)
¡Noche, poesía, locuras de amante! . . .
¡Todo ha de servirnos en esta ocasión!
¡El triunfo es seguro! ¡Valor y adelante!
¿Quién podrá vencernos si es nuestro el amor?

(SILVIA *y* LEANDRO, *abrazados, se dirigen muy despacio a la primera derecha.* CRISPÍN *los sigue sin ser visto por ellos. El telón va bajando muy despacio.*)

TELÓN

The cloak of night mysteriously bereaves
The garden of its hues; when darkness deep
Makes of the flowers mere fragrance, of the leaves
Mere whispers, lovers sweetly long to weep.
The voice that sighs, the voice that loudly sings,
The voice that babbles amorous phrases there
Seem, in the sacred night, like impious things,
A blasphemy that interrupts a prayer.
O soul of silence, whom I venerate,
Your silence speaks the yearnings, ne'er expressed,
Of those who died of love but hid their state,
Who, dying, locked their love within their breast;
Of those who, living, held us far too dear,
So that their words of love could not flow free!
Tonight, is it not *their* voice that I hear
Speaking of love but meaning eternity?
Mother of my soul, the light of yonder star,
Which trembles like a tear of infinite love
Amid the night: is it not, from afar,
The light of *your* eyes in the sky above?
To her whom now I love say merely this:
In all the world I've loved no one but you,
And, since your death, I've only known the kiss
That in the light of yonder star shines through!

LEANDER:
Mother of my soul, the truth is this:
In all the world I've loved no one but you,
And, since your death, I've only known the kiss
That in the light of yonder star shines through!

(*They remain silent, embracing and gazing at each other.*)

CRISPIN: (*appearing from the second wing-space, left; aside*):
Poetry! Night! The nonsense lovers say!
In this affair, all these must be our guide!
Our triumph is assured! On to the fray!
Who'll conquer us when love is on our side?

(SYLVIA *and* LEANDER, *in embrace, move very slowly to the first wing-space, right.* CRISPIN *follows them without being seen by them. The curtain descends very slowly.*)

CURTAIN

Acto segundo

Cuadro tercero

Sala en casa de LEANDRO

Escena I

CRISPÍN, *el* CAPITÁN, ARLEQUÍN. *Salen por la segunda derecha, o sea el pasillo*

CRISPÍN.—Entrad, caballeros, y sentaos con toda comodidad. Diré que os sirvan algo . . . ¡Hola! ¡Eh! ¡Hola!

CAPITÁN.—De ningún modo. No aceptamos nada.

ARLEQUÍN.—Sólo venimos a ofrecernos a tu señor, después de lo que hemos sabido.

CAPITÁN.—¡Increíble traición, que no quedará sin castigar! ¡Yo te aseguro que si el señor Polichinela se pone al alcance de mi mano! . . .

ARLEQUÍN.—¡Ventaja de los poetas! Yo siempre le tendré al alcance de mis versos . . . ¡Oh! La tremenda sátira que pienso dedicarle . . . ¡Viejo dañino, viejo malvado!

CAPITÁN.—¿Y dices que tu amo no fué siquiera herido?

CRISPÍN.—Pero pudo ser muerto. ¡Figuraos! Una docena de espadachines asaltándole de improviso! Gracias a su valor, a su destreza, a mis voces . . .

ARLEQUÍN.—¿Y ello sucedió anoche, cuando tu señor hablaba con Silvia por la tapia de su jardín?

CRISPÍN.—Ya mi señor había tenido aviso . . . : pero ya le conocéis: no es hombre para intimidarse por nada.

CAPITÁN.—Pero debió advertirnos . . .

ARLEQUÍN.—Debió advertir al señor Capitán. Él le hubiera acompañado gustoso.

Act Two

Third Tableau

Parlor in LEANDRO*'s house.*

Scene I

CRISPIN, *the* CAPTAIN, *and* HARLEQUIN *enter from the second wing-space, right, or the corridor.*

CRISPIN: Come in, gentlemen; sit down and make yourselves comfortable. I'll have them serve you something. . . . Ho there! Hey! Hello!

CAPTAIN: By no means. We won't accept a thing.

HARLEQUIN: We've only come to offer our services to your master, after hearing that report.

CAPTAIN: An unbelievable piece of treachery, which won't go unpunished! I assure you that, if Mr. Punchinello comes within reach of my hands . . . !

HARLEQUIN: That's the advantage poets have! I'll always have him within reach of my verses. . . . Oh, the tremendous satire I intend to write about him. . . . Pestiferous old man! Wicked old man!

CAPTAIN: And you say your master wasn't even wounded?

CRISPIN: No, but he might have been killed. Just imagine! A dozen ruffians attacking him with swords unexpectedly! Thanks to his bravery and skill, and to my shouts for help . . .

HARLEQUIN: And this happened last night, while your master was conversing with Sylvia across her garden wall?

CRISPIN: My master had already been warned . . . but you know him by now: he isn't a man to be intimidated by anything.

CAPTAIN: But he should have let us know . . .

HARLEQUIN: He should have informed the Captain. He would have been glad to accompany him.

CRISPÍN.—Ya conocéis a mi señor. Él solo se basta.

CAPITÁN.—¿Y dices que por fin conseguiste atrapar por el cuello a uno de los malandrines, que confesó que todo estaba preparado por el señor Polichinela para deshacerse de tu amo? . . .

CRISPÍN.—¿Y quién sino él podía tener interés en ello? Su hija ama a mi señor; él trata de casarla a su gusto; mi señor estorba sus planes, y el señor Polichinela supo toda su vida cómo suprimir estorbos. ¿No enviudó dos veces en poco tiempo? ¿No heredó en menos a todos sus parientes, viejos y jóvenes? Todos lo saben, nadie dirá que le calumnio . . . ¡Ah! La riqueza del señor Polichinela es un insulto a la humanidad y a la justicia. Sólo entre gente sin honor puede triunfar impune un hombre como el señor Polichinela.

ARLEQUÍN.—Dices bien. Y yo en mi sátira he de decir todo eso . . . Claro que sin nombrarle, porque la poesía no debe permitirse tanta licencia.

CRISPÍN.—¡Bastante le importará a él de vuestra sátira!

CAPITÁN.—Dejadme, dejadme a mí, que como él se ponga al alcance de mi mano . . . Pero bien sé que él no vendrá a buscarme.

CRISPÍN.—Ni mi señor consentiría que se ofendiera al señor Polichinela. A pesar de todo, es el padre de Silvia. Lo que importa es que todos sepan en la ciudad cómo mi amo estuvo a punto de ser asesinado, cómo no puede consentirse que ese viejo zorro contraríe la voluntad y el corazón de su hija.

ARLEQUÍN.—No puede consentirse; el amor está sobre todo.

CRISPÍN.—Y si mi amo fuera algún ruin sujeto . . . Pero, decidme: ¿no es el señor Polichinela el que debía enorgullecerse de que mi señor se haya dignado enamorarse de su hija y aceptarle por suegro? ¡Mi señor, que a tantas doncellas de linaje excelso ha despreciado, y por quien más de cuatro princesas hicieron cuatro mil locuras! . . . Pero ¿quién llega? (*Mirando hacia la segunda derecha.*) ¡Ah Colombina! ¡Adelante, graciosa Colombina, no hayas temor! (*Sale* COLOMBINA.) Todos somos amigos, y nuestra mutua amistad te defiende de nuestra unánime admiración.

CRISPIN: You know my master. He's self-sufficient.

CAPTAIN: And you say he finally managed to grab one of those scoundrels by the collar, and the fellow confessed that the whole thing had been arranged by Mr. Punchinello to get rid of your master? . . .

CRISPIN: Well, who else could be concerned in the matter? His daughter loves my master; *he's* trying to marry her off the way he likes; my master disturbs his plans, and all his life Mr. Punchinello has known how to suppress disturbances. Didn't he twice become a widower in no time at all? Didn't he become the heir, in even less time, of all his relatives, young and old? Everybody knows it, no one will say I'm slandering him. . . . Ah, Mr. Punchinello's wealth is an insult to humanity and justice. Only among people without honor could a man like Mr. Punchinello triumph with impunity.

HARLEQUIN: You're right. And I'm going to say all that in my satire. . . . Without naming him, naturally, because poetry shouldn't allow itself such liberties.

CRISPIN: A lot he'll care about your satire!

CAPTAIN: Let me, let me take care of it, because the moment he comes within reach of my hands . . . But I'm well aware that he won't come looking for me.

CRISPIN: Nor would my master allow Mr. Punchinello to be affronted. In spite of everything, he's Sylvia's father. The important thing is for everyone in town to hear that my master was at the point of being murdered, and that it's intolerable for that old fox to oppose his daughter's wishes and her heart.

HARLEQUIN: It's intolerable; love is above all else.

CRISPIN: As if my master were some nobody . . . But, tell me, isn't Mr. Punchinello the one who should be proud that my master deigned to fall in love with his daughter and accept him as a father-in-law? My master, who has scorned so many young ladies of the highest lineage, and for whom loads of princesses have committed any number of follies! . . . But who's coming? (*Looking toward the second wing-space, right:*) Ah, Columbine! Come in, gracious Columbine, have no fear![12] (COLUMBINE *enters.*) We're all friends, and our mutual friendship protects you from our unanimous admiration.

12. In the Spanish, *no hayas temor* is an archaism for *no tengas temor* or *no temas.*

Escena II

DICHOS *y* COLOMBINA, *que sale por la segunda derecha, o sea el pasillo*

COLOMBINA.—Doña Sirena me envía a saber de tu señor. Apenas rayaba el día, vino Silvia a nuestra casa, y refirió a mi señora todo lo sucedido. Dice que no volverá a casa de su padre, ni saldrá de casa de mi señora más que para ser la esposa del señor Leandro.

CRISPÍN.—¿Eso dice? ¡Oh noble joven! ¡Oh corazón amante!

ARLEQUÍN.—¡Qué epitalamio pienso componer a sus bodas!

COLOMBINA.—Silvia cree que Leandro está malherido . . . Desde su balcón oyó ruido de espadas, tus voces en demanda de auxilio. Después cayó sin sentido, y así la hallaron al amanecer. Decidme lo que sea del señor Leandro, pues muere de angustia hasta saberlo, y mi señora también quedó en cuidado.

CRISPÍN.—Dile que mi señor pudo salvarse, porque amor le guardaba; dile que sólo de amor muere con incurable herida . . . Dile . . . (*Viendo venir a* LEANDRO.) ¡Ah! Pero aquí llega él mismo, que te dirá cuanto yo pudiera decirte.

Escena III

DICHOS *y* LEANDRO, *que sale por la primera derecha*

CAPITÁN.—(*Abrazándole.*) ¡Amigo mío!

ARLEQUÍN.—(*Abrazándole.*) ¡Amigo y señor!

COLOMBINA.—¡Ah señor Leandro! ¡Que estáis salvo! ¡Qué alegría!

LEANDRO.—¿Cómo supisteis?

COLOMBINA.—En toda la ciudad no se habla de otra cosa; por las calles se reúne la gente en corrillos, y todos murmuran y claman contra el señor Polichinela.

LEANDRO.—¿Qué decís?

CAPITÁN.—¡Y si algo volviera a intentar contra vos! . . .

ARLEQUÍN.—¿Y si aún quisiera oponerse a vuestros amores?

COLOMBINA.—Todo sería inútil. Silvia está en casa de mi señora, y sólo saldrá de allí para ser vuestra esposa . . .

LEANDRO.—¿Silvia en vuestra casa? Y su padre . . .

COLOMBINA.—El señor Polichinela hará muy bien en ocultarse.

Scene II

The above and COLUMBINE, *who enters from the second wing-space, right, or the corridor.*

COLUMBINE: I've been sent by Madam Sirena to get news of your master. Scarcely had the day dawned when Sylvia came to our house and reported all the events to my mistress. She says she won't go back to her father's house, or leave my mistress's house except as the bride of Lord Leander.

CRISPIN: She said that? Oh, noble young lady! Oh, what a loving heart!

HARLEQUIN: What an epithalamium I intend to write for their wedding!

COLUMBINE: Sylvia believes that Leander is wounded. . . . From her balcony she heard the clashing of swords and your shouts for help. Then she fainted away, and she was found in that condition at daybreak. Tell me how Lord Leander is doing, because she's dying of worry until she hears something, and my mistress is anxious as well.

CRISPIN: Tell her that my master escaped with his life because love was looking after him; tell her that he's dying of an incurable wound from love alone. . . . Tell her . . . (*Seeing* LEANDER *coming:*) Ah, but here he comes himself, and he'll tell you all that I might have.

Scene III

The above and LEANDER, *who enters from the first wing-space, right.*

CAPTAIN (*hugging him*): My friend!

HARLEQUIN (*hugging him*): My friend and lord!

COLUMBINE: Ah, Lord Leander! So you're safe and sound1 What joy!

LEANDER: How did you find out?

COLUMBINE: All over town no one's talking about anything else; people are gathering in knots in the streets, all grumbling and crying out against Mr. Punchinello.

LEANDER: What's this you say?

CAPTAIN: What if he should make another attempt on your life . . . !

HARLEQUIN: What if he still wants to thwart your romance?

COLUMBINE: It would all be in vain. Sylvia is in my mistress's house, and will only leave it to become your bride. . . .

LEANDER: Sylvia in your house? And her father . . .

COLUMBINE: Mr. Punchinello would be very wise to go into hiding.

CAPITÁN.—¡Creyó que a tanto podría atreverse con su riqueza insolente!

ARLEQUÍN.—Pudo atreverse a todo, pero no al amor . . .

COLOMBINA.—¡Pretender asesinaros tan villanamente!

CRISPÍN.—¡Doce espadachines, doce . . . ; yo los conté!

LEANDRO.—Yo sólo pude distinguir a tres o cuatro.

CRISPÍN.—Mi señor concluirá por deciros que no fué tanto el riesgo, por no hacer mérito de su serenidad y de su valor . . . ¡Pero yo lo vi! Doce eran, doce, armados hasta los dientes, decididos a todo. ¡Imposible me parece que escapara con vida!

COLOMBINA.—Corro a tranquilizar a Silvia y a mi señora.

CRISPÍN.—Escucha, Colombina. A Silvia, ¿no fuera mejor no tranquilizarla? . . .

COLOMBINA.—Déjalo a cargo de mi señora. Silvia cree a estas horas que tu señor está moribundo, y aunque doña Sirena finge contenerla . . . , no tardará en venir aquí sin reparar en nada.

CRISPÍN.—Mucho fuera que tu señora no hubiera pensado en todo.

CAPITÁN.—Vamos también, pues ya en nada podemos aquí serviros. Lo que ahora conviene es sostener la indignación de las gentes contra el señor Polichinela.

ARLEQUÍN.—Apedrearemos su casa . . . Levantaremos a toda la ciudad en contra suya . . . Sepa que si hasta hoy nadie se atrevió contra él, hoy todos juntos nos atreveremos; sepa que hay un espíritu y una conciencia en la multitud.

COLOMBINA.—Él mismo tendrá que venir a rogaros que toméis a su hija por esposa.

CRISPÍN.—Sí, sí; corred, amigos. Ved que la vida de mi señor no está segura . . . El que una vez quiso asesinarle, no se detendrá por nada.

CAPITÁN.—No temáis . . . ¡Amigo mío!

ARLEQUÍN.—¡Amigo y señor!

COLOMBINA.—¡Señor Leandro!

LEANDRO.—Gracias a todos, amigos míos, amigos leales. (*Se van todos, menos* LEANDRO *y* CRISPÍN, *por la segunda derecha.*)

CAPTAIN: He thought he could be that bold because of his insolent riches!

HARLEQUIN: He was able to confront everything, but not love. . . .

COLUMBINE: To try to murder you so vulgarly!

CRISPIN: Twelve bravos, twelve; . . . I counted them!

LEANDER: I was only able to make out three or four.

CRISPIN: My master will end up telling you that the risk wasn't so great, to avoid boasting of his coolness and bravery. . . . But I saw it all! There were twelve of them, twelve, armed to the teeth, ready for anything. I find it impossible that he got away with his life!

COLUMBINE: I'll run and calm down Sylvia and my mistress.

CRISPIN: Listen, Columbine. As for Sylvia, wouldn't it be better not to calm her down?

COLUMBINE: Leave it to my mistress. At this moment Sylvia thinks your master is dying, and, even though Madam Sirena is pretending to restrain her, . . . she'll come here before long, with no regard to any proprieties.

CRISPIN: It would be very surprising if your mistress hadn't thought everything out.

CAPTAIN: We'll leave, too, since we can't be of any service to you here. What counts now is to keep up the people's indignation against Mr. Punchinello.

HARLEQUIN: We'll stone his house. . . . We'll stir up the whole town against him. . . . Rest assured: if up to now nobody dared confront him, today the bunch of us together will have the courage; there's a spirit and a conscience in the masses.

COLUMBINE: He himself will have to come and beseech you to marry his daughter.

CRISPIN: Yes, yes, hurry, my friends! You see that my master's life isn't safe. . . . The man who tried once to murder him won't be restrained by anything.

CAPTAIN: Have no fear. . . . My friend!

HARLEQUIN: My friend and lord!

COLUMBINE: Lord Leander!

LEANDER: My thanks to all of you, my friends, my faithful friends! (*All except* LEANDER *and* CRISPIN *exit into the second wing-space, right.*)

Escena IV

LEANDRO *y* CRISPÍN

LEANDRO.—¿Qué es esto, Crispín? ¿Qué pretendes? ¿Hasta dónde has de llevarme con tus enredos? ¿Piensas que lo creí? Tú pagaste a los espadachines; todo fué invención tuya. ¡Mal hubiera podido valerme contra todos si ellos no vinieran de burla!

CRISPÍN.—¿Y serás capaz de reñirme, cuando así anticipo el logro de tus esperanzas?

LEANDRO.—No, Crispín, no. ¡Bien sabes que no! Amo a Silvia y no lograré su amor con engaños, suceda lo que suceda.

CRISPÍN.—Bien sabes lo que ha de sucederte . . . ¡Si amar es resignarse a perder lo que se ama por sutilezas de conciencia . . . , que Silvia misma no ha de agradecerte! . . .

LEANDRO.—¿Qué dices? ¡Si ella supiera quién soy!

CRISPÍN.—Y cuando lo sepa, ya no serás el que fuiste: serás su esposo, su enamorado esposo, todo lo enamorado y lo fiel y lo noble que tú quieras y ella puede desear . . . Una vez dueño de su amor . . . , y de su dote, ¿no serás el más perfecto caballero? Tú no eres como el señor Polichinela, que con todo su dinero, que tantos lujos le permite, aún no se ha permitido el lujo de ser honrado . . . En él es naturaleza la truhanería; pero en ti, en ti fué sólo necesidad . . . Y aun si no me hubieras tenido a tu lado, ya te hubieras dejado morir de hambre de puro escrupuloso. ¡Ah! ¿Crees que si yo hubiera hallado en ti otro hombre me hubiera contentado con dedicarte a enamorar? . . . No; te hubiera dedicado a la política, y no al dinero del señor Polichinela; el mundo hubiera sido nuestro . . . Pero no eres ambicioso, te contentas con ser feliz . . .

LEANDRO.—Pero ¿no viste que mal podía serlo? Si hubiera mentido para ser amado y ser rico de este modo, hubiera sido porque yo no amaba, y mal podía ser feliz. Y si amo, ¿cómo puedo mentir?

CRISPÍN.—Pues no mientas. Ama, ama con todo tu corazón, inmensamente. Pero defiende tu amor sobre todo. En amor no es mentir callar lo que puede hacernos perder la estimación del ser amado.

LEANDRO.—Ésas sí que son sutilezas, Crispín.

CRISPÍN.—Que tú debiste hallar antes si tu amor fuera como dices. Amor es todo sutileza, y la mayor de todas no es engañar a los demás, sino engañarse a sí mismo.

Scene IV

LEANDER *and* CRISPIN

LEANDER: What's all this, Crispin? What do you have in mind? What are you leading me into with your stratagems? Do you think I believed it? You paid those ruffians; the whole thing was your idea. I'd scarcely have been able to fend all of them off if they weren't just faking it!

CRISPIN: And you have the heart to scold me when, by so doing, I bring your hopes closer to fulfillment?

LEANDER: No, Crispin, no. You know it's not so! I love Sylvia and I won't win her love with deceitful tricks, no matter what happens.

CRISPIN: You know very well what will happen to you. . . . If loving means resigning yourself to lose what you love out of minute scruples of conscience, . . . Sylvia herself won't thank you for it! . . .

LEANDER: What are you saying? If she were to find out what I really am!

CRISPIN: By the time she finds out, you'll no longer be the man you were: you'll be her husband, her loving husband, as loving, faithful, and noble as you could wish and she could desire. . . . Once you're in possession of her love—and her dowry—won't you be the most perfect gentleman? You're not like Mr. Punchinello, who, with all his money, which allows him so many luxuries, has not yet allowed himself the luxury of being honorable. . . . In him, being a scoundrel is second nature; but in you, in you it was merely a result of necessity. . . . And, what's more, if you hadn't had me with you, you would have let yourself die of hunger long ago, just by being so scrupulous. Ah! Do you think that, if I had found a different man in you, I'd have been satisfied merely to set you up as a lover? . . . No; I would have dedicated you to politics, and not to Mr. Punchinello's money; the world would have been at our feet. . . . But you aren't ambitious, you're contented with being happy. . . .

LEANDER: But didn't you see that I could hardly become happy? If I had told lies in order to be loved and rich in this way, it would have been because I wasn't really in love, and so I could hardly become happy. And now that I *am* in love, how can I tell lies?

CRISPIN: Then don't lie. Love, love with your whole heart, immeasurably. But protect your love above all. In love, it isn't lying to keep quiet about things that might make us lose the esteem of the loved one.

LEANDER: Those are just hair-splitting subtleties, Crispin.

CRISPIN: —Which you should have discovered long before this, if your love was as strong as you say. Love is nothing *but* subtle stratagems, and the chief one of all isn't to deceive other people, but to deceive yourself.

LEANDRO.—Yo no puedo engañarme, Crispín. No soy de esos hombres que cuando venden su conciencia se creen en el caso de vender también su entendimiento.

CRISPÍN.—Por eso dije que no servías para la política. Y bien dices. Que el entendimiento es la conciencia de la verdad, y el que llega a perderla entre las mentiras de su vida, es como si se perdiera a sí propio, porque ya nunca volverá a encontrarse ni a conocerse, y él mismo vendrá a ser otra mentira.

LEANDRO.—¿Dónde aprendiste tanto, Crispín?

CRISPÍN.—Medité algún tiempo en galeras, donde esta conciencia de mi entendimiento me acusó más de torpe que de pícaro. Con más picardía y menos torpeza, en vez de remar en ellas pude haber llegado a mandarlas. Por eso juré no volver en mi vida. Piensa de qué no seré capaz ahora que por tu causa me veo a punto de quebrantar mi juramento.

LEANDRO.—¿Qué dices?

CRISPÍN.—Que nuestra situación es ya insostenible, que hemos apurado nuestro crédito, las gentes ya empiezan a pedir algo efectivo. El hostelero, que nos albergó con toda esplendidez por muchos días, esperando que recibieras tus libranzas. El señor Pantalón, que, fiado en el crédito del hostelero, nos proporcionó cuanto fué preciso para instalarnos con suntuosidad en esta casa . . . Mercaderes de todo género, que no dudaron en proveernos de todo, deslumbrados por tanta grandeza. Doña Sirena misma, que tan buenos oficios nos ha prestado en tus amores . . . Todos han esperado lo razonable, y sería injusto pretender más de ellos, ni quejarse de tan amable gente . . . ¡Con letras de oro quedará grabado en mi corazón el nombre de esta insigne ciudad que desde ahora declaro por mi madre adoptiva! A más de éstos . . . , ¿olvidas que de otras partes habrán salido y andarán en busca nuestra? ¿Piensas que las hazañas de Mantua y de Florencia son para olvidarlas? ¿Recuerdas el famoso proceso de Bolonia? . . . ¡Tres mil doscientos folios sumaban cuando nos ausentamos alarmados de verle crecer tan sin tino! ¿Qué no habrá aumentado bajo la pluma de aquel gran doctor jurista que le había tomado por su cuenta? ¡Qué de considerandos y de resultandos de que no resultará cosa buena! ¿Y aún dudas? ¿Y aún me reprendes porque di la batalla que puede decidir en un día de nuestra suerte?

LEANDRO.—¡Huyamos!

CRISPÍN.—¡No! ¡Basta de huir a la desesperada! Hoy ha de fijarse nuestra fortuna . . . Te di el amor, dame tú la vida.

LEANDER: I can't deceive myself, Crispin. I'm not one of those men who, when they sell their conscience, feel compelled to sell their good sense as well.

CRISPIN: That's why I said you weren't suitable for politics. And you're right. Because good sense is the awareness of truth, and whoever comes to lose it amid the falsehoods of his life is like a man who's lost his own self, because he'll never again encounter himself or know himself, and he himself will become just another lie.

LEANDER: Where did you learn all that, Crispin?

CRISPIN: I meditated for some time in the galleys, where this awareness of my good sense revealed I was more dimwitted than rascally. With more rascality and less dimwittedness, instead of rowing in them I might have come to command them. And so I swore never to return as long as I lived. Just think what I may not do, now that, on your account, I find myself on the verge of breaking my oath.

LEANDER: What do you mean?

CRISPIN: That by now our situation is untenable, that we've used up our credit and people are beginning to ask for cash. The innkeeper, who lodged us quite splendidly for many days, waiting for you to receive your remittances. Mr. Pantaloon, who, trusting in the innkeeper's confidence, furnished us with all we needed to settle sumptuously in this house. . . . Merchants of every kind, who didn't hesitate to provide us with everything, dazzled as they were by our lofty station. Even Madam Sirena, who was so helpful to us in your romance. . . . They've all waited a reasonable time, and it would be unfair to expect more from them or to complain about such amiable people. . . . The name of this excellent city—which, from here on, I declare to be my adoptive mother—will remain engraved in my heart with golden letters! Besides the locals, . . . have you forgotten that people elsewhere have probably sallied forth and are searching for us? Do you think that our doings in Mantua and Florence are of the forgettable kind? Do you remember that well-known criminal investigation in Bologna? The dossier amounted to thirty-two hundred folio sheets when we slipped away, alarmed to see it grow so immoderately! How big must it be by now, as compiled by that eminent doctor of law who had taken charge of it? All those "in consideration of which"-es and "as a result of which"-es that will never lead to any good result! And you still doubt me? And you still reproach me for engaging in the battle that may decide our fate in one day?

LEANDER: Let's escape!

CRISPIN: No! Enough of running away in despair! Today our fortune is to be determined. . . . I've given you love, now you give me life!

LEANDRO.—Pero ¿cómo salvarnos? ¿Qué puedo yo hacer? Dime.

CRISPÍN.—Nada ya. Basta con aceptar lo que los demás han de ofrecernos. Piensa que hemos creado muchos intereses y es interés de todos el salvarnos.

Escena V

DICHOS *y* DOÑA SIRENA, *que sale por la segunda derecha, o sea el pasillo*

SIRENA.—¿Dais licencia, señor Leandro?

LEANDRO.—¡Doña Sirena! ¿Vos en mi casa?

SIRENA.—Ya veis a lo que me expongo. A tantas lenguas maldicientes. ¡Yo en casa de un caballero, joven, apuesto!

CRISPÍN.—Mi señor sabría hacer callar a los maldicientes si alguno se atreviera a poner sospechas en vuestra fama.

SIRENA.—¿Tu señor? No me fío. ¡Los hombres son tan jactanciosos! Pero en nada reparo por serviros. ¿Qué me decís, señor, que anoche quisieron daros muerte? No se habla de otra cosa . . . ¡Y Silvia! ¡Pobre niña! ¡Cuánto os ama! ¡Quisiera saber qué hicisteis para enamorarla de ese modo!

CRISPÍN.—Mi señor sabe que todo lo debe a vuestra amistad.

SIRENA.—No diré yo que no me deba mucho . . . que siempre hablé de él como yo no debía, sin conocerle lo bastante . . . A mucho me atreví por amor vuestro. Si ahora faltáis a vuestras promesas . . .

CRISPÍN.—¿Dudáis de mi señor? ¿No tenéis cédula firmada de su mano? . . .

SIRENA.—¡Buena mano y buen nombre! ¿Pensáis que todos no nos conocemos? Yo sé confiar y sé que el señor Leandro cumplirá como debe. Pero si vierais que hoy es un día aciago para mí, y por lograr hoy una mitad de lo que se me ha ofrecido, perdería gustosa la otra mitad . . .

CRISPÍN.—¿Hoy decís?

SIRENA.—¡Día de tribulaciones! Para que nada falte, veinte años hace hoy también que perdí a mi segundo marido, que fué el primero, el único amor de mi vida.

CRISPÍN.—Dicho sea en elogio del primero.

SIRENA.—El primero me fué impuesto por mi padre. Yo no le amaba, y a pesar de ello supe serle fiel.

LEANDER: But how can we be rescued? What can I do? Tell me.

CRISPIN: By now, nothing. It's enough to accept what the others have to offer us. Remember that we've created many bonds of interest, and it's in everyone's interest to rescue us.

Scene V

The above and MADAM SIRENA, *who enters from the second wing-space, right, or the corridor.*

SIRENA: May I come in, Lord Leander?

LEANDER: Madam Sirena! You in my house?

SIRENA: You see what I'm exposing myself to. To all those slanderous tongues. I in the house of a young, elegant gentleman!

CRISPIN: My master would be able to shut any slanderous mouth if anyone dared to lay your reputation open to suspicion.

SIRENA: Your master? I don't trust him. Men are so boastful! But, in order to serve you, I disregard all conventions. Tell me, sir, did someone try to kill you last night? No one's talking about anything else. . . . And Sylvia! Poor child! How she loves you! I'd like to know what you did to make her love you so!

CRISPIN: My master knows that he owes it all to your friendship.

SIRENA: I won't deny that he owes me a lot . . . because I've always talked about him as I perhaps shouldn't have, not knowing him sufficiently well. . . . I went out on a limb for your sake. And if you now fail to make good on your promises . . .

CRISPIN: You doubt my master? Don't you possess a document that he signed with his own hand? . . .

SIRENA: A fine hand and a fine name! Don't you think we all know one another? I know whom to trust, and I know that Lord Leander will pay up as he ought to. But if you only knew: today is an unlucky day for me, and if I could put my hands today on half of what you offered me, I'd gladly forego the other half. . . .

CRISPIN: Today, you say?

SIRENA: A day of tribulations! And to top it all off, it's twenty years today since I lost my second husband, who was the first, the only love of my life.

CRISPIN: Which says a lot for your first husband.

SIRENA: The first one was forced on me by my father. I didn't love him, but in spite of that I managed to be faithful to him.

CRISPÍN.—¿Qué no sabréis vos, doña Sirena?

SIRENA.—Pero dejemos los recuerdos, que todo lo entristecen. Hablemos de esperanzas. ¿Sabéis que Silvia quiso venir conmigo?

LEANDRO.—¿Aquí, a esta casa?

SIRENA.—¿Qué os parece? ¿Qué diría el señor Polichinela? ¡Con toda la ciudad soliviantada contra él, fuerza le sería casaros!

LEANDRO.—No, no; impedidla que venga.

CRISPÍN.—¡Chis! Comprenderéis que mi señor no dice lo que siente.

SIRENA.—Lo comprendo . . . ¿Qué no daría él por ver a Silvia a su lado, para no separarse nunca de ella?

CRISPÍN.—¿Qué daría? ¡No lo sabéis!

SIRENA.—Por eso lo pregunto.

CRISPÍN.—¡Ah doña Sirena! . . . Si mi señor es hoy esposo de Silvia, hoy mismo cumplirá lo que os prometió.

SIRENA.—¿Y si no lo fuera?

CRISPÍN.—Entonces . . . , lo habréis perdido todo. Ved lo que os conviene.

LEANDRO.—¡Calla, Crispín! ¡Basta! No puedo consentir que mi amor se trate como mercancía. Salid, doña Sirena, decid a Silvia que vuelva a casa de su padre, que no venga aquí en modo alguno, que me olvide para siempre, que yo he de huir donde no vuelva a saber de mi nombre . . . ¡Mi nombre! ¿Tengo yo nombre acaso?

CRISPÍN.—¿No callarás?

SIRENA.—¿Qué le dió? ¡Qué locura es ésta! ¡Volved en vos! ¡Renunciar de ese modo a tan gran ventura! . . . Y no se trata sólo de vos. Pensad que hay quien todo lo fió en vuestra suerte, y no puede burlarse así de una dama de calidad que a tanto se expuso por serviros. Vos no haréis tal locura; vos o caseréis con Silvia, o habrá quien sepa pediros cuenta de vuestros engaños, que no estoy tan sola en el mundo como pudisteis creer, señor Leandro.

CRISPÍN.—Doña Sirena dice muy bien. Pero creed que mi señor sólo habla así ofendido por vuestra desconfianza.

SIRENA.—No es desconfianza en él . . . Es, todo he de decirlo . . . , es que el señor Polichinela no es hombre de dejarse burlar . . . , y ante el clamor que habéis levantado contra él con vuestra estratagema de anoche . . .

CRISPÍN.—¿Estratagema decís?

SIRENA.—¡Bah! Todos nos conocemos. Sabed que uno de los es-

CRISPIN: What can't you manage to do, Madam Sirena?

SIRENA: But let's set aside memories, which make everything so sad. Let's talk about our hopes. Do you know that Sylvia wanted to come with me?

LEANDER: Here, to this house?

SIRENA: What do you think of that? What would Mr. Punchinello say? With the whole town up in arms against him, he'd be compelled to give you her hand!

LEANDER: No, no; stop her from coming!

CRISPIN: Sh! You realize that my master isn't saying what he really feels.

SIRENA: I understand. . . . What wouldn't he give to see Sylvia beside him, never more to be parted from her?

CRISPIN: What he'd give? You don't know!

SIRENA: That's why I'm asking.

CRISPIN: Ah, Madam Sirena! . . . If my master becomes Sylvia's husband today, this very day he'll fulfill his promises to you.

SIRENA: And if he doesn't?

CRISPIN: Then . . . you'll have lost everything. Now decide what you ought to do.

LEANDER: Quiet, Crispin! Enough! I can't allow my love to be dealt with like merchandise. Go out, Madam Sirena, tell Sylvia to return to her father's house, and by no means to come here; let her forget me forever, because I will flee where she'll never hear my name again. . . . My name! Do I have a name, by any chance?

CRISPIN: Won't you keep still?

SIRENA: What's got into him? What folly this is! Pull yourself together! To give up such good luck this way! . . . And you're not the only one involved. Remember that others have entrusted their all to your good fortune; you can't make such a mockery of a lady of quality who has taken such risks in your service. You won't commit such a folly; either you'll marry Sylvia, or someone will take you to account for your confidence tricks, because I'm not so alone in the world as you might have thought, Lord Leander.

CRISPIN: Madam Sirena is perfectly right. But, trust me, my master is talking this way merely because he was hurt by your mistrust.

SIRENA: It isn't mistrust in him. . . . The reason is—I've got to come out with it all—the reason is that Mr. Punchinello isn't a man to let himself be fooled, . . . and, in the face of the outcry you've stirred up against him by your stratagem last night . . .

CRISPIN: A stratagem, you call it?

SIRENA: Bah! We all know one another. Let me inform you that one

padachines es pariente mío, y los otros me son también muy allegados . . . Pues bien: el señor Polichinela no se ha descuidado, y ya se murmura por la ciudad que ha dado aviso a la Justicia de quién sois y cómo puede perderos; dícese también que hoy llegó de Bolonia un proceso . . .

CRISPÍN.—¡Y un endiablado doctor con él! Tres mil novecientos folios . . .

SIRENA.—Todo esto se dice, se asegura. Ved si importa no perder tiempo.

CRISPÍN.—¿Y quién lo malgasta y lo pierde sino vos? Volved a vuestra casa . . . Decid a Silvia . . .

SIRENA.—Silvia está aquí. Vino junto con Colombina, como otra doncella de mi acompañamiento. En vuestra antecámara espera. Le dije que estabais muy malherido . . .

LEANDRO.—¡Oh Silvia mía!

SIRENA.—Sólo pensó en que podíais morir . . . , nada pensó en lo que arriesgaba con venir a veros. ¿Soy vuestra amiga?

CRISPÍN.—Sois adorable. Pronto. Acostaos aquí, haceos el doliente y el desmayado. Ved que si es preciso yo sabré que lo estéis de veras. (*Amenazándole y haciéndole sentar en un sillón.*)

LEANDRO.—Sí, soy vuestro; lo sé, lo veo . . . Pero Silvia no lo será. Sí, quiero verla; decidle que llegue, que he de salvarla a pesar vuestro, a pesar de todos, a pesar de ella misma.

CRISPÍN.—Comprenderéis que mi señor no siente lo que dice.

SIRENA.—No lo creo tan necio ni tan loco. Ven conmigo. (*Se va con* CRISPÍN *por la segunda derecha, o sea el pasillo.*)

Escena VI

LEANDRO *y* SILVIA, *que sale por la segunda derecha*

LEANDRO.—¡Silvia! ¡Silvia mía!

SILVIA.—¿No estás herido?

LEANDRO.—No; ya lo ves . . . Fué un engaño, un engaño más para traerte aquí. Pero no temas: pronto vendrá tu padre; pronto saldrás con él sin que nada tengas tú que reprocharme . . . ¡Oh! Sólo el haber empañado la serenidad de tu alma con una ilusión de amor, que para ti sólo será el recuerdo de un mal sueño.

SILVIA.—¿Qué dices, Leandro? ¿Tu amor no era verdad?

of those ruffians is a relative of mine and the others are closely connected to me as well. . . . Well, then: Mr. Punchinello hasn't let things slide, and there's already a rumor in town that he's tipped off the police to who you are and how they can ruin you; it's also said that a judicial dossier has arrived from Bologna today. . . .

CRISPIN: And a diabolical doctor of the law along with it! Thirty-nine hundred folio sheets . . .

SIRENA: All of that is being said, and told for a certainty. Consider whether or not it's important to lose no time!

CRISPIN: Well, who's wasting and losing it except you? Go back home. . . . Tell Sylvia—

SIRENA: Sylvia's here. She came along with Columbine, as another one of the young ladies escorting me. She's waiting in your antechamber. I told her you were badly wounded. . . .

LEANDER: Oh, my Sylvia!

SIRENA: Her only thought was that you might die; . . . she gave no thought to what she was risking by coming to see you. Am I a friend of yours?

CRISPIN: You're marvelous. (*To* LEANDER:) Quick! Rest here, pretend to be in pain and in a faint. Remember: if necessary, I'll see to it that you really are! (*Threatening him and making him sit in an armchair.*)

LEANDER: Yes, I'm in your hands; I know it, I see it. . . . But Sylvia won't be. Yes, I want to see her; tell her to come, because I'm going to save her in spite of you, in spite of everyone, in spite of herself.

CRISPIN: You realize that my master doesn't really feel what he's saying.

SIRENA: I don't think he's that foolish or that crazy. Come with me. (*She exits with* CRISPIN *into the second wing-space, right, or the corridor.*)

Scene VI

LEANDER *and* SYLVIA, *who enters from the second wing-space, right.*

LEANDER: Sylvia! My Sylvia!

SYLVIA: You're not wounded?

LEANDER: No, as you can see. . . . It was a trick, one more trick to get you here. But have no fear; your father will soon come; soon you'll leave with him and you'll have nothing to reproach me for—oh! except for clouding the brightness of your soul with a false hope of love, which for you will be merely the recollection of a bad dream.

SYLVIA: What are you saying, Leander? Your love wasn't true?

LEANDRO.—¡Mi amor, sí . . . ; por eso no he de engañarte! Sal de aquí pronto, antes de que nadie, fuera de los que aquí te trajeron, pueda saber que viniste.

SILVIA.—¿Qué temes? ¿No estoy segura en tu casa? Yo no dudé en venir a ella . . . ¿Qué peligros pueden amenazarme a tu lado?

LEANDRO.—Ninguno; dices bien. Mi amor te defiende de tu misma inocencia.

SILVIA.—No he de volver a casa de mi padre después de su acción horrible.

LEANDRO.—No, Silvia, no culpes a tu padre. No fué él; fué otro engaño más, otra mentira . . . Huye de mí, olvida a este miserable aventurero, sin nombre, perseguido por la Justicia.

SILVIA.—¡No, no es cierto! Es que la conducta de mi padre me hizo indigna de vuestro cariño. Eso es. Lo comprendo . . . ¡Pobre de mí!

LEANDRO.—¡Silvia! ¡Silvia mía! ¡Qué crueles tus dulces palabras! ¡Qué cruel esa noble confianza de tu corazón, ignorante del mal y de la vida!

Escena VII

DICHOS *y* CRISPÍN, *que sale corriendo por la segunda derecha*

CRISPÍN.—¡Señor! ¡Señor! El señor Polichinela llega.

SILVIA.—¡Mi padre!

LEANDRO.—¡Nada importa! Yo os entregaré a él por mi mano.

CRISPÍN.—Ved que no viene solo, sino con mucha gente y justicia con él.

LEANDRO.—¡Ah! ¡Si te hallan aquí! ¡En mi poder! Sin duda tú les diste aviso . . . Pero no lograréis vuestro propósito.

CRISPÍN.—¿Yo? No por cierto . . . Que esto va de veras, y ya temo que nadie pueda salvarnos.

LEANDRO.—¡A nosotros no; ni he de intentarlo! . . . Pero a ella sí. Conviene ocultarle; queda aquí.

SILVIA.—¿Y tú?

LEANDRO.—Nada temas. ¡Pronto, que llegan! (*Esconde a* SILVIA *en la habitación del foro, diciéndole a* CRISPÍN:) Tú verás lo que trae a esa

LEANDER: My love *was;* . . . that's why I won't deceive you! Leave this place quickly, before anyone except those who brought you here can find out that you came.

SYLVIA: What are you afraid of? Am I not safe in your house? I didn't hesitate to come here. . . . What dangers can threaten me when I'm with you?

LEANDER: None; you're right. My love protects you from your very innocence.

SYLVIA: I won't go back to my father's house after the horrible thing he did.

LEANDER: No, Sylvia, don't blame your father. He didn't do it; it was one more trick, one more lie. . . . Flee my presence, forget this abject adventurer, nameless, wanted by the police.

SYLVIA: No, it isn't so! It's because my father's conduct has made me unworthy of your affection. That's why. I understand. . . . How unhappy I am!

LEANDER: Sylvia! My Sylvia! How cruel your sweet words are! How cruel that noble trustingness of your heart, which knows nothing of evil and real life!

Scene VII

The above and CRISPIN, *who runs in from the second wing-space, right.*

CRISPIN: Master! Master! Mr. Punchinello is coming!

SYLVIA: My father!

LEANDER: It makes no difference! I'll hand you over to him personally.

CRISPIN: Please observe that he isn't coming alone, but with a lot of people, including police.

LEANDER: Ah, if they find you here! In my hands! (*To* CRISPIN:) I'm sure you tipped them off. . . . But you won't achieve your aims!

CRISPIN: I? No, indeed. . . . Because this is no trick, and now I fear that nobody can save us.

LEANDER: Us, no! And I won't even try! But her, yes. We must hide her; stay here.

SYLVIA: And you?

LEANDER: Have no fear. Quick, they're coming! (*He hides* SYLVIA *in the room at the rear of the stage, saying to* CRISPIN:) Go see what

gente. Sólo cuida de que nadie entre ahí hasta mi regreso . . . No hay otra huída. (*Se dirige a la ventana.*)

CRISPÍN.—(*Deteniéndole.*) ¡Señor! ¡Tente! No te mates así!

LEANDRO.—No pretendo matarme ni pretendo escapar; pretendo salvarla. (*Trepa hacia arriba por la escalera y desaparece.*)

CRISPÍN.—¡Señor, señor! ¡Menos mal! Creí que intentaba arrojarse al suelo, pero trepó hacia arriba . . . Esperemos todavía . . . Aún quiere volar . . . Es su región, las alturas. Yo, a la mía: la tierra . . . Ahora más que nunca conviene afirmarse en ella. (*Se sienta en un sillón con mucha calma.*)

Escena VIII

CRISPÍN, *el* SEÑOR POLICHINELA, *el* HOSTELERO, *el* SEÑOR PANTALÓN, *el* CAPITÁN, ARLEQUÍN, *el* DOCTOR, *el* SECRETARIO *y dos* ALGUACILES *con enormes protocolos de curia. Todos salen por la segunda derecha, o sea el pasillo*

POLICHINELA.—(*Dentro, a gente que se supone fuera.*) ¡Guardad bien las puertas, que nadie salga, hombre ni mujer, ni perro ni gato!

HOSTELERO.—¿Dónde están, dónde están esos bandoleros, esos asesinos?

PANTALÓN.—¡Justicia! ¡Justicia! ¡Mi dinero! ¡Mi dinero! (*Van saliendo todos por el orden que se indica. El* DOCTOR *y el* SECRETARIO *se dirigen a la mesa y se disponen a escribir. Los dos* ALGUACILES, *de pie, teniendo en las manos enormes protocolos del proceso.*)

CAPITÁN.—Pero, ¿es posible lo que vemos, Crispín?

ARLEQUÍN.—¿Es posible lo que sucede?

PANTALÓN.—¡Justicia! ¡Justicia! ¡Mi dinero! ¡Mi dinero!

HOSTELERO.—¡Que los prendan . . . , que se aseguren de ellos!

PANTALÓN.—¡No escaparán . . . , no escaparán!

CRISPÍN.—Pero, ¿qué es esto? ¿Cómo se atropella así la mansión de un noble caballero? Agradezcan la ausencia de mi señor.

PANTALÓN.—¡Calla, calla, que tú eres su cómplice y has de pagar con él!

HOSTELERO.—¿Cómo cómplice? Tan delincuente como su pretendido señor . . . , que él fué quien me engañó.

CAPITÁN.—¿Qué significa esto, Crispín?

ARLEQUÍN.—¿Tiene razón esta gente?

POLICHINELA.—¿Qué dices ahora, Crispín? ¿Pensaste que habían

those people want. Only, take care that no one comes in here until I'm back. . . . There's no other way out. (*He heads toward the window.*)

CRISPIN (*holding him back*): Master! Stop! Don't kill yourself!

LEANDER: I don't intend to kill myself, and I don't intend to escape; I intend to save her. (*He climbs up the steps and is lost to sight.*)

CRISPIN: Master, master! Good! I thought he was trying to hurl himself to the ground, but he climbed up. . . . Let's wait a while longer. . . . He still wants to fly. . . . The heights are his region. Let me get to mine: down to earth. . . . Now more than ever I need to get a steady footing on it. (*He sits down in an armchair with perfect calm.*)

Scene VIII

CRISPIN, MR. PUNCHINELLO, *the* INNKEEPER, MR. PANTALOON, *the* CAPTAIN, HARLEQUIN, *the* DOCTOR, *his* SECRETARY, *and two* CONSTABLES *with an enormous amount of legal papers. All (but* CRISPIN*) enter from the second wing-space, right, or the corridor.*

PUNCHINELLO (*within, to people presumed to be outside*): Guard the doors carefully; no one is to leave, neither man nor woman, dog nor cat!

INNKEEPER: Where are they, where are those bandits, those assassins?

PANTALOON: Justice, justice! My money! My money! (*They all enter in the order indicated above. The* DOCTOR *and his* SECRETARY *head for the table and get ready to write. The two* CONSTABLES *stand on their feet, holding an enormous amount of trial documents.*)

CAPTAIN: But, Crispin, is what we see possible?

HARLEQUIN: Is what's happening possible?

PANTALOON: Justice, justice! My money! My money!

INNKEEPER: Arrest them! Don't let them get away!

PANTALOON: They won't escape, . . . they won't escape!

CRISPIN: But what's all this? How can you barge into a noble lord's mansion this way? You should be glad my master is out.

PANTALOON: Quiet, quiet! You're his accomplice, and you're going to pay like him!

INNKEEPER: What do you mean, accomplice? He's as big a criminal as his so-called master, . . . because he's the one who tricked me.

CAPTAIN: What does this mean, Crispin?

HARLEQUIN: Are these people right?

PUNCHINELLO: What do you say now, Crispin? Did you imagine that

de valerte tus enredos conmigo? ¿Conque yo pretendí asesinar a tu señor? ¿Conque yo soy un viejo avaro que sacrifica a su hija? ¿Conque toda la ciudad se levanta contra mí llenándome de insultos? Ahora veremos.

PANTALÓN.—Dejadle, señor Polichinela, que éste es asunto nuestro, que al fin vos no habéis perdido nada. Pero yo . . . , ¡todo mi caudal, que lo presté sin garantía! ¡Perdido me veré para toda la vida! ¿Qué será de mí?

HOSTELERO.—¿Y yo, decidme, que gasté lo que no tenía y aun hube de empeñarme por servirle como creí correspondía a su calidad? ¡Esto es mi destrucción, mi ruina!

CAPITÁN.—¡Y nosotros también fuimos ruinmente engañados! ¿Qué se dirá de mí, que puse mi espada y mi valor al servicio de un aventurero?

ARLEQUÍN.—¿Y de mí, que le dediqué soneto tras soneto como al más noble señor?

POLICHINELA.—¡Ja, ja, ja!

PANTALÓN.—¡Sí, reíd, reíd! . . . Como nada perdisteis . . .

HOSTELERO.—Como nada os robaron . . .

PANTALÓN.—¡Pronto, pronto! ¿Dónde está el otro pícaro?

HOSTELERO.—Registradlo todo hasta dar con él.

CRISPÍN.—Poco a poco. Si dais un solo paso . . . (*Amenazando con la espada.*)

PANTALÓN.—¿Amenazas todavía? ¿Y esto ha de sufrirse? ¡Justicia, justicia!

HOSTELERO.—¡Eso es, justicia!

DOCTOR.—Señores . . . Si no me atendéis, nada conseguiremos. Nadie puede tomarse justicia por su mano, que la justicia no es atropello ni venganza y *summum jus, summa injuria*. La justicia es todo sabiduría, y la sabiduría es todo orden, y el orden es todo razón, y la razón es todo procedimiento, y el procedimiento es todo lógica. *Barbara, Celarent, Darii, Ferioque, Barilapton,* depositad en mí vuestros agravios y querellas, que todo ha de unirse a este proceso que conmigo traigo.

CRISPÍN.—¡Horror! ¡Aún ha crecido!

DOCTOR.—Constan aquí otros muchos delitos de estos hombres, y a ellos han de sumarse estos de que ahora les acusáis. Y yo seré

your stratagems would work with me? And so, I tried to murder your master? And so, I'm an old skinflint who's sacrificing his daughter? And so, the whole town rises up against me, heaping insults on me? Now we'll see.

PANTALOON: Let him alone, Mr. Punchinello; this is our business, because, after all, you haven't lost a thing. But I . . . my whole fortune, which I loaned without security! I'll be ruined for the rest of my life! What's to become of me?

INNKEEPER: And what about me, tell me? I spent money I didn't have and even went into debt in order to wait on him in a manner that I thought befitted his rank! This is my destruction, my downfall!

CAPTAIN: And we, too, were basely deceived! What will people say about me, I who devoted my sword and my valor to the service of an adventurer?

HARLEQUIN: And about me, I who dedicated one sonnet after another to him as if he were the most noble lord?

PUNCHINELLO: Ha, ha, ha!

PANTALOON: Yes, laugh, laugh! . . . Seeing that you haven't lost anything. . . .

INNKEEPER: Since you weren't robbed of anything. . . .

PANTALOON: Quick, quick! Where's the other delinquent?

INNKEEPER: Search everywhere until he's found!

CRISPIN: Take it easy! If you take even one step . . . (*Threatening with his sword.*)

PANTALOON: Still making threats? Are we to put up with this? Justice, justice!

INNKEEPER: Yes, justice!

DOCTOR: Gentlemen . . . If you don't heed me, we'll accomplish nothing. No one can take the law into his own hands, because the law is neither outrageous behavior nor vengeance, and *summum jus, summa injuria.*[13] The law is entirely wisdom, and wisdom is entirely order, and order is entirely reason, and reason is entirely procedure, and procedure is entirely logic. *Barbara, Celarent, Darii, Ferioque, Barilapton.*[14] Leave in my charge all your grievances and complaints, because they must all be added to these investigation papers that I have brought with me.

CRISPIN: My heavens! There are even more of them now!

DOCTOR: Many other crimes committed by these men are recorded here, and the ones of which you now accuse them must be added to

13. "Law carried to an extreme is the height of injustice." A quotation from Cicero's *De officiis* (*On Official Duties*). 14. Mnemonic terms, meaningless in themselves, referring to the modes of the syllogism in medieval Scholastic logic.

parte en todos ellos; sólo así obtendréis la debida satisfacción y justicia. Escribid, señor Secretario, y vayan deponiendo los querellantes.

PANTALÓN.—Dejadnos de embrollos, que bien conocemos vuestra justicia.

HOSTELERO.—No se escriba nada, que todo será poner lo blanco negro. Y quedaremos nosotros sin nuestro dinero y ellos sin castigar.

PANTALÓN.—Eso, eso . . . ¡Mi dinero, mi dinero! ¡Y después justicia!

DOCTOR.—¡Gente indocta, gente ignorante, gente incivil! ¿Qué idea tenéis de la justicia? No basta que os digáis perjudicados si no pareciese bien claramente que hubo intención de causaros perjuicio, esto es, fraude o dolo, que no es lo mismo . . . aunque la vulgar aceptación los confunda. Pero sabed . . . , que en el un caso . . .

PANTALÓN.—¡Basta! ¡Basta! Que acabaréis por decir que fuimos nosotros los culpables.

DOCTOR.—¡Y como pudiera ser si os obstináis en negar la verdad de los hechos! . . .

HOSTELERO.—¡Ésta es buena! Que fuimos robados. ¿Qué más verdad ni más claro delito?

DOCTOR.—Sabed que robo no es lo mismo que hurto; y mucho menos que fraude o dolo, como dije primero. Desde las Doce Tablas hasta Justiniano, Triboniano, Emiliano y Triberiano . . .

PANTALÓN.—Todo fué quedarnos sin nuestro dinero . . . Y de ahí no habrá quien nos saque.

POLICHINELA.—El señor Doctor habla muy en razón. Confiad en él, y que todo conste en proceso.

DOCTOR.—Escribid, escribid luego, señor Secretario.

CRISPÍN.—¿Quieren oírme?

PANTALÓN.—¡No, no! Calle el pícaro . . . , calle el desvergonzado.

HOSTELERO.—Ya hablaréis donde os pesará.

DOCTOR.—Ya hablará cuando le corresponda, que a todos ha de oírse en justicia . . . Escribid, escribid. En la ciudad de . . . , a tantos

the others. And I will be the investigating judge for all of them; only in this way will you obtain the satisfaction and justice that are due to you. Secretary, write, and let the plaintiffs make their depositions.

PANTALOON: Leave us out of your entanglements; we're quite familiar with your brand of justice.

INNKEEPER: Let nothing be written down, for it will only mean turning black into white. And we'll be left without our money, and they without their punishment.

PANTALOON: Right, right! . . . My money, my money! And justice later on!

DOCTOR: Uncouth, ignorant, and uncivil people! What's your conception of the law? It isn't enough for you to say you've suffered damage; there has to be clear evidence that an intention to cause you detriment existed—that is, fraud or misrepresentation, which aren't the same thing, . . . although common parlance confuses them. But I'll have you know that in the one case—

PANTALOON: Enough, enough! You'll end up saying that *we* were the guilty parties.

DOCTOR: Which might be the case if you stubbornly deny the truth of the facts! . . .

INNKEEPER: That's a fine thing! We were robbed. What can be more true or a more evident crime?

DOCTOR: I'll have you know that robbery is not the same as theft; they're much less alike than fraud and misrepresentation, which I mentioned earlier. From the time of the Twelve Tables down to Justinian, Tribonian, Aemilian, and Triberian—[15]

PANTALOON: It was nothing but leaving us without our money. . . . And nobody will be able to change *that* situation.

PUNCHINELLO: The Doctor is speaking quite reasonably. Trust him, and let all your testimony be added to the investigation dossier.

DOCTOR: So then, write, write, Secretary.

CRISPIN: Are you willing to hear me out?

PANTALOON: No, no! Let the rogue hold his tongue, . . . let that shameless fellow keep still!

INNKEEPER: You'll have a chance to speak in a place you won't like.

DOCTOR: He'll speak at the proper time, because in law everyone must be heard. . . . Write, write. In the city of —, on the date of —. It

15. The Twelve Tables were ancient Roman legislation of the fifth century B.C. Tribonian presided over the committee that drew up the celebrated law code, *Corpus juris civilis*, of Byzantine emperor Justinian (reigned 527–565). Aemilian and Triberian would appear to be fictitious names.

. . . No sería malo proceder primeramente al inventario de cuanto hay en la casa.

CRISPÍN.—No dará tregua a la pluma . . .

DOCTOR.—Y proceder al depósito de fianza por parte de los querellantes, porque no pueda haber sospecha en su buena fe. Bastará con dos mil escudos de presente y caución de todos sus bienes.

PANTALÓN.—¿Qué decís? ¡Nosotros dos mil escudos!

DOCTOR.—Ocho debieran ser; pero basta que seáis personas de algún crédito para que todo se tenga en cuenta, que nunca fuí desconsiderado . . .

HOSTELERO.—¡Alto, y no se escriba más, que no hemos de pasar por eso!

DOCTOR.—¿Cómo? ¿Así se atropella a la Justicia? Ábrase proceso separado por violencia y mano airada contra un ministro de Justicia en funciones de su ministerio.

PANTALÓN.—¡Este hombre ha de perdernos!

HOSTELERO.—¡Está loco!

DOCTOR.—¿Hombre y loco, decís? Hablen con respeto. Escribid, escribid que hubo también ofensas de palabra . . .

CRISPÍN.—Bien os está por no escucharme.

PANTALÓN.—Habla, habla, que todo será mejor, según vemos.

CRISPÍN.—Pues atajen a ese hombre, que levantará monte con sus papelotes.

PANTALÓN.—¡Basta, basta ya, decimos!

HOSTELERO.—Deje la pluma . . .

DOCTOR.—Nadie sea osado a poner mano en nada.

CRISPÍN.—Señor Capitán, sírvanos vuestra espada, que es también atributo de justicia.

CAPITÁN.—(*Va a la mesa y da un fuerte golpe con la espada en los papeles que está escribiendo el* DOCTOR.) Háganos la merced de no escribir más.

DOCTOR.—Ved lo que es pedir las cosas en razón. Suspended las actuaciones, que hay cuestión previa a dilucidar . . . Hablen las partes entre sí . . . Bueno fuera, no obstante, proceder en el ínterin al inventario . . .

PANTALÓN.—¡No, no!

DOCTOR.—Es formalidad que no puede evitarse.

CRISPÍN.—Ya escribiréis cuando sea preciso. Dejadme ahora hablar aparte con estos honrados señores.

DOCTOR.—Si os conviene sacar testimonio de cuanto aquí les digáis . . .

wouldn't be a bad idea to start off by taking an inventory of everything in the house.

CRISPIN: He won't let his pen take a rest. . . .

DOCTOR: And to proceed with the security deposit on the part of the plaintiffs, so that there can be no doubts about their good faith. It will be enough if they pay two thousand crowns immediately and put up all their property as collateral.

PANTALOON: What's that you say? We are to pay two thousand crowns?

DOCTOR: It ought to be eight, but since you're clearly reliable people, I'll take that into account, because I've never been inconsiderate. . . .

INNKEEPER: Stop right there, and don't write any more, because we aren't going to submit to that!

DOCTOR: What? Is this how you trample on the law? Let a separate investigation be initiated, for violence and hands raised in anger against a servant of the law during the performance of his duties.

PANTALOON: This fellow is going to ruin us!

INNKEEPER: He's crazy!

DOCTOR: "Fellow" and "crazy," you said? Speak respectfully. Write that down, write down that there was also offensive language. . . .

CRISPIN: That's what you deserve for not listening to me.

PANTALOON: Talk, talk, because anything would be better than this; we see that now.

CRISPIN: In that case, interrupt that man before his papers grow as high as a mountain.

PANTALOON: Enough, enough now, we say!

INNKEEPER: Drop that pen! . . .

DOCTOR: Let no one be so bold as to lay hands on anything!

CRISPIN: Captain, let your sword be at our service; it, too, is an attribute of the law.

CAPTAIN (*going to the table and bringing his sword down hard on the papers on which the* DOCTOR *is writing*): Be so good as to stop writing.

DOCTOR: You see how helpful it is to make a reasonable request! Suspend the proceedings, because there's a previous question to be elucidated. . . . Let the parties confer with each other. . . . Nevertheless, it would be a good idea to get on with the inventory in the interim. . . .

PANTALOON: No, no!

DOCTOR: It's a formality that can't be avoided.

CRISPIN: You'll write when it's necessary. Now let me talk in private with these honorable gentlemen.

DOCTOR: If you want what you say to them to be entered as testimony . . .

CRISPÍN.—Por ningún modo. No se escriba una letra, o no hablaré palabra.

CAPITÁN.—Deje hablar al mozo.

CRISPÍN.—¿Y qué he de deciros? ¿De qué os quejáis? ¿De haber perdido vuestro dinero? ¿Qué pretendéis? ¿Recobrarlo?

PANTALÓN.—¡Eso, eso! ¡Mi dinero!

HOSTELERO.—¡Nuestro dinero!

CRISPÍN.—Pues escuchadme aquí . . . ¿De dónde habéis de cobrarlo si así quitáis crédito a mi señor y así hacéis imposible su boda con la hija del señor Polichinela? ¡Voto a . . . , que siempre pedí tratar con pícaros mejor que con necios! Ved lo que hicisteis y cómo se compondrá ahora con la Justicia de por medio. ¿Qué lograréis ahora si dan con nosotros en galeras o en sitio peor? ¿Será buena moneda para cobraros los túrdigas de nuestro pellejo? ¿Seréis más ricos, más nobles o más grandes cuando nosotros estemos perdidos? En cambio, si no nos hubierais estorbado a tan mal tiempo, hoy, hoy mismo tendríais vuestro dinero, con todos sus intereses . . . , que ellos solos bastarían a llevaros a la horca, si la Justicia no estuviera en esas manos y en esas plumas . . . Ahora haced lo que os plazca, que ya os dije lo que os convenía . . .

DOCTOR.—Quedaron suspensos . . .

CAPITÁN.—Yo aún no puedo creer que ellos sean tales bellacos.

POLICHINELA.—Este Crispín . . . capaz será de convencerlos.

PANTALÓN.—(*Al* HOSTELERO.) ¿Qué decís a esto? Bien mirado . . .

HOSTELERO.—¿Qué decís vos?

PANTALÓN.—Dices que hoy mismo se hubiera casado tu amo con la hija del señor Polichinela. ¿Y si él no da su consentimiento? . . .

CRISPÍN.—De nada ha de servirle. Que su hija huyó con mi señor . . . y lo sabrá todo el mundo . . . y a él más que a nadie importa que nadie sepa cómo su hija se perdió por un hombre sin condición, perseguido por la Justicia.

PANTALÓN.—Si así fuera . . . ¿Qué decís vos?

HOSTELERO.—No nos ablandaremos. Ved que el bellaco es maestro en embustes.

PANTALÓN.—Decís bien. No sé cómo pude creerlo. ¡Justicia! ¡Justicia!

CRISPIN: By no means! Not a single letter must be written down, or else I won't say a word.

CAPTAIN: Let the fellow speak.[16]

CRISPIN: And what do I have to say to you? What are you complaining about? About having lost your money? What is it you want? To get it back?

PANTALOON: Yes, yes! My money!

INNKEEPER: Our money!

CRISPIN: Then, listen to me here. . . . How can you get it back if you invalidate my master's credit this way, thus making it impossible for him to marry Mr. Punchinello's daughter? By God, I've always preferred to deal with scoundrels rather than with fools! Consider what you've done, and how things can now be settled, with the law intervening. What will you now accomplish if they throw us into the galleys or some place worse? Will the strips of skin lashed off of us be good money restored to you? Will you be richer, nobler, or greater when we are ruined? On the other hand, if you hadn't disturbed us at such a bad time, today, this very day you would have your money, with all accrued interest—which alone would be enough to send you to the gallows, if the law didn't reside in *those* hands and *those* pens. . . . Now do whatever you like, because I've now told you what's good for you. . . .

DOCTOR: He's left them bewildered. . . .

CAPTAIN: I still can't believe that they're such rogues.

PUNCHINELLO: This Crispin . . . may be capable of persuading them.

PANTALOON (*to the* INNKEEPER): What do you say to this? When you consider it carefully . . .

INNKEEPER: What do *you* say?

PANTALOON: You say that this very day your master would have married Mr. Punchinello's daughter. What if he doesn't give his consent? . . .

CRISPIN: It will do him no good. Because his daughter has eloped with my master . . . and the whole world will soon know it . . . and it concerns him more than anyone else that no one should find out how his daughter ruined herself for a man of no standing, a fugitive from the law.

PANTALOON: If that's true . . . What do *you* say?

INNKEEPER: Let's not get softened up. Remember, this rogue is a master of slyness.

PANTALOON: You're right. I don't know how I came to believe him. Justice! Justice!

16. Obviously, Crispin has now withdrawn to a corner of the room with his creditors, and cannot be heard by Punchinello or the lawmen. Later on, the dialogue indicates who has heard what at any given time.

CRISPÍN.—¡Ved que lo perdéis todo!

PANTALÓN.—Veamos todavía . . . Señor Polichinela, dos palabras.

POLICHINELA.—¿Qué me queréis?

PANTALÓN.—Suponed que nosotros no hubiéramos tenido razón para quejarnos. Suponed que el señor Leandro fuera, en efecto, el más noble caballero . . . , incapaz de una baja acción . . .

POLICHINELA.—¿Qué decís?

PANTALÓN.—Suponed que vuestra hija le amara con locura, hasta el punto de haber huído con él de vuestra casa.

POLICHINELA.—¿Que mi hija huyó de mi casa con ese hombre? ¿Quién lo dijo? ¿Quién fué el desvergonzado? . . .

PANTALÓN.—No os alteréis. Todo es suposición.

POLICHINELA.—Pues aun así no he de tolerarlo.

PANTALÓN.—Escuchad con paciencia. Suponed que todo eso hubiera sucedido. ¿No os sería forzoso casarla?

POLICHINELA.—¿Casarla? ¡Antes la mataría! Pero es locura pensarlo. Y bien veo que eso quisierais para cobraros a costa mía, que sois otros tales bribones. Pero no será, no será . . .

PANTALÓN.—Ved lo que decís, y no se hable aquí de bribones cuando estáis presente.

HOSTELERO.—¡Eso, eso!

POLICHINELA.—¡Bribones, bribones, combinados para robarme! Pero no será, no será.

DOCTOR.—No hayáis cuidado, señor Polichinela, que aunque ellos renunciaren a perseguirle, ¿no es nada este proceso? ¿Creéis que puede borrarse nada de cuanto en él consta, que son cincuenta y dos delitos probados y otros tantos que no necesitan probarse? . . .

PANTALÓN.—¿Qué decís ahora, Crispín?

CRISPÍN.—Que todos esos delitos, si fueran tantos, son como estos otros . . . Dinero perdido que nunca se pagará si nunca le tenemos.

DOCTOR.—¡Eso no! Que yo he de cobrar lo que me corresponda de cualquier modo que sea.

CRISPÍN.—Pues será de los que se quejaron, que nosotros harto haremos en pagar con nuestras personas.

DOCTOR.—Los derechos de Justicia son sagrados, y lo primero será embargar para ellos cuanto hay en esta casa.

PANTALÓN.—¿Cómo es eso? Esto será para cobrarnos algo.

HOSTELERO.—Claro es; y de otro modo . . .

CRISPIN: Be careful, you're ruining everything!

PANTALOON: Let's look further into this. . . . Mr. Punchinello, a word with you.

PUNCHINELLO: What do you want of me?

PANTALOON: Just suppose that we were wrong to bring a complaint. Just suppose that Lord Leander was really the most noble gentleman, . . . incapable of a low action. . . .

PUNCHINELLO: What do you mean?

PANTALOON: Just suppose that your daughter loved him madly, to the extent of leaving your house and eloping with him.

PUNCHINELLO: My daughter run away from my house with that man? Who said so? Who was so shameless? . . .

PANTALOON: Don't get angry. It's all a supposition.

PUNCHINELLO: Well, even so, I won't tolerate it.

PANTALOON: Hear me out patiently. Suppose that all of that had happened. Wouldn't you be compelled to marry her off?

PUNCHINELLO: Marry her off? I'd kill her first! But even the idea is insane. And I realize that you'd like it to happen so you could get your money back at my expense, because you're a bunch of crooks. But it won't happen, it won't happen. . . .

PANTALOON: Watch what you're saying, and let there be no talk of crooks here while *you're* around.

INNKEEPER: Right, right!

PUNCHINELLO: Crooks, crooks, in cahoots to rob me! But it won't happen, it won't happen.

DOCTOR: Don't worry, Mr. Punchinello, because even if they drop their own complaints, is this dossier nothing? Do you think anything recorded in it can be expunged? It includes fifty-two proven crimes and the same number which don't need to be proved.

PANTALOON: What do you say to that, Crispin?

CRISPIN: That all those crimes, even if they add up to that many, are just like the rest of them. . . . Lost money which will never be paid if we never get any.

DOCTOR: There you're wrong! Because I must be paid what's coming to me, no matter how.

CRISPIN: Then it will have to come from the plaintiffs, because we'll have all we can do to pay with our bodies.

DOCTOR: Legal fees are sacrosanct, and my first act will be to seize everything in this house so they can be paid.

PANTALOON: How's that? That would get us back something.

INNKEEPER: Naturally; otherwise . . .

DOCTOR.—Escribid, escribid, que si hablan todos nunca nos entenderemos.

PANTALÓN y HOSTELERO.—¡No, no!

CRISPÍN.—Oídme aquí, señor Doctor. Y si se os pagara de una vez y sin escribir tanto vuestros . . . , ¿cómo los llamáis? ¿Estipendios?

DOCTOR.—Derechos de Justicia.

CRISPÍN.—Como queráis. ¿Qué os parece?

DOCTOR.—En ese caso . . .

CRISPÍN.—Pues ved que mi amo puede ser hoy rico, poderoso, si el señor Polichinela consiente en casarle con su hija. Pensad que la joven es hija única del señor Polichinela; pensad en que mi señor ha de ser dueño de todo; pensad . . .

DOCTOR.—Puede, puede estudiarse.

PANTALÓN.—¿Qué os dijo?

HOSTELERO.—¿Qué resolvéis?

DOCTOR.—Dejadme reflexionar. El mozo no es lerdo y se ve que no ignora los procedimientos legales. Porque si consideramos que la ofensa que recibisteis fué puramente pecuniaria y que todo delito que puede ser reparado en la misma forma lleva en la reparación el más justo castigo; si consideramos que así en la ley bárbara y primitiva del Talión se dijo: ojo por ojo, diente por diente, mas no diente por ojo ni ojo por diente . . . Bien puede decirse en este caso escudo por escudo. Porque al fin, él no os quitó la vida para que podáis exigir la suya en pago. No os ofendió en vuestra persona, honor ni buena fama, para que podáis exigir otro tanto. La equidad es la suprema justicia. *Equitas justitia magna est.* Y desde las Pandectas hasta Triboniano, con Emiliano, Triberiano . . .

PANTALÓN.—No digáis más. Si él nos pagara . . .

HOSTELERO.—Como él nos pagara . . .

POLICHINELA.—¡Qué disparates son éstos, y cómo ha de pagar, ni qué tratar ahora!

CRISPÍN.—Se trata de que todos estáis interesados en salvar a mi señor, en salvarnos por interés de todos. Vosotros, por no perder vuestro dinero; el señor Doctor, por no perder toda esa suma de admirable doctrina que fuisteis depositando en esa balumba de sabiduría; el señor Capitán, porque todos le vieron amigo de mi amo, y a su valor importa que no se murmure de su amistad con un aventurero; vos, señor Arlequín, porque vuestros ditirambos de poeta perderían todo

DOCTOR: Write, write this down, because if everyone speaks, we'll never reach an understanding.

PANTALOON and INNKEEPER: No, no!

CRISPIN: Listen to me now, Doctor. What if we could avoid writing so much, and you could be paid at once all of your—what do you call them? Stipends?

DOCTOR: Legal fees.

CRISPIN: As you like. What do you think about that?

DOCTOR: In that case . . .

CRISPIN: Then, consider that today my master can be rich and powerful if Mr. Punchinello consents to his marriage to his daughter. Recall that the young lady is Mr. Punchinello's only child; recall that my master would come into possession of everything; recall—

DOCTOR: This is an aspect worthy of reflection.

PANTALOON: What did he say to you?

INNKEEPER: What's your decision?

DOCTOR: Let me think. The fellow is far from dimwitted and he's obviously familiar with legal proceedings. Because if we take into account that the harm done to you was purely pecuniary, and that any crime for which amends can be made in the same form receives its most just punishment in those very amends; if we take into account that the barbarous and primitive law of retaliation stated "An eye for an eye, a tooth for a tooth," but not "a tooth for an eye" or "an eye for a tooth" . . . One may well say in this case: "a coin for a coin." Because, after all, he didn't take your life, allowing you to claim *his* in return. He didn't harm you physically, or injure your honor or reputation, allowing you to exact the same thing from him. Fairness is the highest justice. *Equitas justitia magna est.* And from the Pandects[17] down to Tribonian, along with Aemilian, Triberian, . . .

PANTALOON: Say no more. If he were to pay us . . .

INNKEEPER: As long as he pays us . . .

PUNCHINELLO: This is all nonsense! How can he pay, and what's the point of negotiating now?

CRISPIN: The point is that everyone has an interest in rescuing my master, in rescuing us in everyone's interest. Both of *you*, so that you don't lose your money; you, Doctor, so you don't lose that great mass of admirable learning that you've been entering into that huge heap of wisdom; the Captain, because everyone saw his friendship with my master, and it's essential to his honor to avoid rumors that he abetted an adventurer; you, Mr. Harlequin, because your poetic dithyrambs would

17. A digest of ancient Roman legal decisions and opinions.

su mérito al saber que tan mal los empleasteis; vos, señor Polichinela . . . , antiguo amigo mío, porque vuestra hija es ya ante el Cielo y ante los hombres la esposa del señor Leandro.

POLICHINELA.—¡Mientes, mientes! ¡Insolente, desvergonzado!

CRISPÍN.—Pues procédase al inventario de cuanto hay en la casa. Escribid, escribid, y sean todos estos señores testigos y empiécese por este aposento. (*Descorre el tapiz de la puerta del foro y aparecen formando grupo* SILVIA, LEANDRO, DOÑA SIRENA, COLOMBINA *y la* SEÑORA DE POLICHINELA.)

Escena IX

DICHOS, SILVIA, LEANDRO, DOÑA SIRENA, COLOMBINA *y la* SEÑORA DE POLICHINELA, *que aparece por el foro*

PANTALÓN y HOSTELERO.—¡Silvia!

CAPITÁN y ARLEQUÍN.—¡Juntos! ¡Los dos!

POLICHINELA.—¿Conque era cierto? ¡Todos contra mí! ¡Y mi mujer y mi hija con ellos! ¡Todos conjurados para robarme! ¡Prended a ese hombre, a esas mujeres, a ese impostor, o yo mismo . . . !

PANTALÓN.—¿Estáis loco, señor Polichinela?

LEANDRO.—(*Bajando al proscenio en compañía de los demás.*) Vuestra hija vino aquí creyéndome malherido acompañada de doña Sirena, y yo mismo corrí al punto en busca de vuestra esposa para que también la acompañara. Silvia sabe quién soy, sabe toda mi vida de miserias, de engaños, de bajezas, y estoy seguro que de nuestro sueño de amor nada queda en su corazón . . . Llevadla de aquí, llevadla; yo os lo pido antes de entregarme a la justicia.

POLICHINELA.—El castigo de mi hija es cuenta mía; pero a ti . . . ¡Prendedle digo!

SILVIA.—¡Padre! Si no le salváis, será mi muerte. Le amo, le amo siempre, ahora más que nunca. Porque su corazón es noble y fué muy desdichado, y pudo hacerme suya con mentir, y no ha mentido.

POLICHINELA.—¡Calla, calla, loca, desvergonzada! Éstas son las enseñanzas de tu madre . . . , sus vanidades y fantasías. Éstas son las lecturas romancescas, las músicas a la luz de la luna.

SEÑORA DE POLICHINELA.—Todo es preferible a que mi hija se case con un hombre como tú, para ser desdichada como su madre. ¿De qué me sirvió nunca la riqueza?

lose all their merit, were it known that you addressed them so misguidedly; you, Mr. Punchinello, . . . my old friend, . . . because in the eyes of Heaven and mankind your daughter is already Lord Leander's wife.

PUNCHINELLO: That's a lie, a lie! Insolent, shameless man!

CRISPIN: Well, then, let's proceed with the inventory of everything in the house. Write it down, write it down, and let all these gentlemen be witnesses—starting with *this* room! (*He draws the drape that covered the entrance to the room at the rear, and, forming a group,* SYLVIA, LEANDER, MADAM SIRENA, COLUMBINE, *and* PUNCHINELLO'S WIFE *are revealed.*)

Scene IX

The above; SYLVIA, LEANDER, MADAM SIRENA, COLUMBINE, *and* PUNCHINELLO'S WIFE, *revealed at the rear of the stage.*

PANTALOON and INNKEEPER: Sylvia!

CAPTAIN and HARLEQUIN: The two together!

PUNCHINELLO: So it was true? Everyone against me! And my wife and daughter along with them! All in cahoots to rob me! Arrest that man, those women, that impostor, or else I myself—!

PANTALOON: Are you crazy, Mr. Punchinello?

LEANDER (*coming down to the proscenium together with the others*): Your daughter came here in the belief that I was wounded. She was chaperoned by Madam Sirena, and I myself immediately ran off to fetch your wife so that she could chaperone her, too. Sylvia knows who I am, she knows my entire life of wretchedness, deceit, and baseness; and I'm sure not a trace of our dream of love is left in her heart. . . . Take her away from here, take her away. I ask this of you before I surrender to the law.

PUNCHINELLO: Punishing my daughter is my affair; but as for you—arrest him, I say!

SYLVIA: Father! If you don't save him it will be the death of me. I love him, I'll always love him, and now more than ever. Because his heart is noble and he's been very unfortunate, and he might have made me his by lying, but he didn't lie.

PUNCHINELLO: Quiet, quiet, you crazy, shameless girl! This is what comes of your mother's teachings, . . . her vanity and fantasies. This is what comes of reading novels and listening to music by moonlight.

PUNCHINELLO'S WIFE: And it's all better than having my daughter marry a man like you, so she can be as unhappy as her mother is. What good did wealth ever do me?

SIRENA.—Decís bien, señora Polichinela. ¿De qué sirven las riquezas sin amor?

COLOMBINA.—De lo mismo que el amor sin riquezas.

DOCTOR.—Señor Polichinela, nada os estará mejor que casarlos.

PANTALÓN.—Ved que esto ha de saberse en la ciudad.

HOSTELERO.—Ved que todo el mundo estará de su parte.

CAPITÁN.—Y no hemos de consentir que hagáis violencia a vuestra hija.

DOCTOR.—Y ha de constar en el proceso que fué hallada aquí, junto con él.

CRISPÍN.—Y en mi señor no hubo más falta que carecer de dinero, pero a él nadie le aventajará en nobleza . . . , y vuestros nietos serán caballeros . . . , si no dan en salir al abuelo . . .

TODOS.—¡Casadlos! ¡Casadlos!

PANTALÓN.—O todos caeremos sobre vos.

HOSTELERO.—Y saldrá a relucir vuestra historia . . .

ARLEQUÍN.—Y nada iréis ganando . . .

SIRENA.—Os lo pide una dama, conmovida por este amor tan fuera de estos tiempos.

COLOMBINA.—Que más parece de novela.

TODOS.—¡Casadlos! ¡Casadlos!

POLICHINELA.—Cásense enhoramala. Pero mi hija quedará sin dote y desheredada . . . Y arruinaré toda mi hacienda antes que ese bergante . . .

DOCTOR.—Eso sí que no haréis, señor Polichinela.

PANTALÓN.—¿Qué disparates son éstos?

HOSTELERO.—¡No lo penséis siquiera!

ARLEQUÍN.—¿Qué se diría?

CAPITÁN.—No lo consentiremos.

SILVIA.—No, padre mío; soy yo la que nada acepto, soy yo la que ha de compartir su suerte. Así le amo.

LEANDRO.—Y sólo así puedo aceptar tu amor . . . (*Todos corren hacia* SILVIA *y* LEANDRO.)

DOCTOR.—¿Qué dicen? ¿Están locos?

PANTALÓN.—¡Eso no puede ser!

HOSTELERO.—¡Lo aceptaréis todo!

ARLEQUÍN.—Seréis felices y seréis ricos.

SEÑORA DE POLICHINELA.—¡Mi hija en la miseria! ¡Ese hombre es un verdugo!

SIRENA.—Ved que el amor es niño delicado y resiste pocas privaciones.

SIRENA: You're right, Mrs. Punchinello. What good is wealth without love?

COLUMBINE: As much good as love without wealth.

DOCTOR: Mr. Punchinello, the best thing you can do is let them marry.

PANTALOON: Consider that this will become known around town.

INNKEEPER: Consider that everyone will be on their side.

CAPTAIN: And we can't allow you to do violence to your daughter.

DOCTOR: And it must be added to my dossier that she was found here in his company.

CRISPIN: And my master's only fault was to have no money; but no one will surpass him in nobility, . . . and your grandchildren will be gentlemen, . . . unless they take after their grandfather. . . .

ALL: Let them marry! Let them marry!

PANTALOON: Or we'll all get after you.

INNKEEPER: And your past history will come to light. . . .

HARLEQUIN: And you'll gain nothing by it. . . .

SIRENA: A lady is requesting you to, a lady whose heart is touched by this love which is so alien to our day and age.

COLUMBINE: It's more like a romance in a novel.

ALL: Let them marry! Let them marry!

PUNCHINELLO: Let them marry and be damned! But my daughter will have no dowry, and I'll disinherit her. . . . And I'll let all my fortune go to rack and ruin before this scoundrel—

DOCTOR: That's exactly what you won't do, Mr. Punchinello.

PANTALOON: What's this nonsense?

INNKEEPER: Don't even think of it!

HARLEQUIN: What would people say?

CAPTAIN: We won't allow it.

SYLVIA: No, father; I'm the one who won't accept a thing, I'm the one who wishes to share his lot. That's how much I love him.

LEANDER: And only under those terms can I accept your love. . . . (*All run up to* SYLVIA *and* LEANDER.)

DOCTOR: What are they saying? Are they crazy?

PANTALOON: This mustn't happen!

INNKEEPER: You'll both accept everything!

HARLEQUIN: You'll be happy and you'll be rich.

PUNCHINELLO'S WIFE: My daughter a pauper! That man is a tyrant!

SIRENA: Remember that love is a delicate child and can't stand many privations.

DOCTOR.—¡No ha de ser! Que el señor Polichinela firmará aquí mismo espléndida donación, como corresponde a una persona de su calidad y a un padre amantísimo. Escribid, escribid, señor Secretario, que a esto no ha de oponerse nadie.

TODOS.—(*Menos* POLICHINELA.) ¡Escribid, escribid!

DOCTOR.—Y vosotros, jóvenes enamorados . . . , resignaos con las riquezas, que no conviene extremar escrúpulos que nadie agradece.

PANTALÓN.—(*A* CRISPÍN.) ¿Seremos pagados?

CRISPÍN.—¿Quién lo duda? Pero habéis de proclamar que el señor Leandro nunca os engañó . . . Ved cómo se sacrifica por satisfaceros aceptando esa riqueza que ha de repugnar sus sentimientos.

PANTALÓN.—Siempre le creímos un noble caballero.

HOSTELERO.—Siempre.

ARLEQUÍN.—Todos lo creímos.

CAPITÁN.—Y lo sostendremos siempre.

CRISPÍN.—Y ahora, Doctor, ese proceso, ¿habrá tierra bastante en la tierra para echarle encima?

DOCTOR.—Mi previsión se anticipa a todo. Bastará con puntuar debidamente algún concepto . . . Ved aquí: donde dice . . . "Y resultando que si no declaró . . . ," basta una coma, y dice: "Y resultando que sí, no declaró . . ." Y aquí: "Y resultando que no, debe condenársele . . . ," fuera la coma, y dice: "Y resultando que no debe condenársele . . ."

CRISPÍN.—¡Oh admirable coma! ¡Maravillosa coma! ¡Genio de la Justicia! ¡Oráculo de la Ley! ¡Monstruo de la Jurisprudencia!

DOCTOR.—Ahora confío en la grandeza de tu señor.

CRISPÍN.—Descuidad. Nadie mejor que vos sabe cómo el dinero puede cambiar a un hombre.

SECRETARIO.—Yo fuí el que puso y quitó esas comas . . .

CRISPÍN.—En espera de algo mejor . . . Tomad esta cadena. Es de oro.

SECRETARIO.—¿De ley?

CRISPÍN.—Vos lo sabréis, que entendéis de leyes.

DOCTOR: It won't happen! Because here and now Mr. Punchinello is going to sign a munificent transfer of property, as befits a man of his standing and a loving father. Write, write, Secretary, for no one is going to oppose this.

ALL (*except* PUNCHINELLO): Write, write!

DOCTOR: And you, the young lovers, resign yourselves to be rich, because it's wrong to be exaggeratedly scrupulous when it's to no one's benefit.

PANTALOON (*to* CRISPIN): Will we be paid?

CRISPIN: Beyond any doubt! But you'll have to announce publicly that Lord Leander never deceived you. . . . See how he sacrifices himself in order to satisfy you, by accepting that wealth, which must be repugnant to his feelings.

PANTALOON: We always believed he was a noble gentleman.

INNKEEPER: Always.

HARLEQUIN: We all believed it.

CAPTAIN: And we'll always maintain it.

CRISPIN: And now, Doctor, that dossier: is there enough earth on Earth to cover it up with?

DOCTOR: My foresight is ahead of you all. All that's needed is to punctuate a few clauses properly. . . . Look here: where it says "The result being no declaration was made to the effect that . . . ," all that's needed is a comma, and it reads "The result being no, declaration was made to the effect that. . . ." And in this place—"The result being no, cause for condemning him exists"—out goes the comma, and it reads "The result being no cause for condemning him exists."[18]

CRISPIN: Oh, admirable comma! Wonderful comma! Genius of justice! Oracle of the law! Prodigy of jurisprudence!

DOCTOR: Now I trust in your master's generosity.

CRISPIN: Never fear. No one knows better than you how money can change a man.

SECRETARY: I'm the one who added and deleted those commas.

CRISPIN: While awaiting something better, . . . take this chain. It's gold.

SECRETARY: Fine?

CRISPIN: You'll surely know: you understand all about fines.[19]

18. A perfectly literal translation cannot give the effect of the original. The exact meaning of the Spanish (devoid of English word-play) will be found in the second part of the Appendix. 19. A paraphrase was necessary to retain the pun. Literally, the Secretary asks: "Is [the gold] pure [OR: standard]?" Crispin replies: "You'll surely know; you understand all about laws."

POLICHINELA.—Sólo impondré una condición: que este pícaro deje para siempre de estar a tu servicio.

CRISPÍN.—No necesitáis pedirlo, señor Polichinela. ¿Pensáis que soy tan pobre de ambiciones como mi señor?

LEANDRO.—¿Quieres dejarme, Crispín? No será sin tristeza de mi parte.

CRISPÍN.—No la tengáis, que ya de nada puedo serviros y conmigo dejáis la piel del hombre viejo . . . ¿Qué os dije, señor? Que entre todos habían de salvarnos . . . Creedlo. Para salir adelante con todo, mejor que crear afectos es crear intereses . . .

LEANDRO.—Te engañas, que sin el amor de Silvia nunca me hubiera salvado.

CRISPÍN.—¿Y es poco interés ese amor? Yo di siempre su parte al ideal y conté con él siempre. Y ahora acabó la farsa.

SILVIA.—(*Al público.*) Y en ella visteis, como en las farsas de la vida, que a estos muñecos, como a los humanos, muévenlos corderillos groseros, que son los intereses, las pasioncillas, los engaños y todas las miserias de su condición: tiran unos de sus pies y los llevan a tristes andanzas; tiran otros de sus manos, que trabajan con pena, luchan con rabia, hurtan con astucia, matan con violencia. Pero entre todos ellos, desciende a veces del cielo al corazón un hilo sutil, como tejido con luz de sol y con luz de luna: el hilo del amor, que a los humanos, como a esos muñecos que semejan humanos, les hace parecer divinos, y trae a nuestra frente resplandores de aurora, y pone alas en nuestro corazón y nos dice que no todo es farsa en la farsa, que hay algo divino en nuestra vida que es verdad y es eterno, y no puede acabar cuando la farsa acaba. (*Telón.*)

FIN DE LA COMEDIA

PUNCHINELLO: I'll impose only one condition: that this scoundrel leaves your service forever.

CRISPIN: You don't need to make that request, Mr. Punchinello. Do you think I'm as unambitious as my master?

LEANDER: You want to leave me, Crispin? It won't be without sadness on my part.

CRISPIN: Don't be sad, because there's nothing further I can do for you, and, with me gone, you can cast off your old criminal skin. . . . Wasn't it as I told you, sir? That they'd all get together to save us. . . . Take my word. To get ahead in the world, it's not so effective to create bonds of affection as it is to create bonds of interest. . . .

LEANDER: You're wrong, because without Sylvia's love I would never have been saved.

CRISPIN: And is that love a negligible interest? I've always given ideals their due, and I've always counted on them. And now the farce is over.

SYLVIA (*to the audience*): And in it, just as in the farces of real life, you've seen that these marionettes, like human beings, are moved by rough strings: their self-interest, their petty passions, deceit, and all the wretchedness of their condition. Some of the strings pull their feet and make them walk on unhappy paths; others pull their hands, which labor with pain, struggle with rage, steal with cunning, and kill with violence. But among them all, at times there descends to their heart from heaven a fine thread, as if spun out of sunlight and moonlight: the thread of love, which makes human beings, like these marionettes which resemble human beings, seem to be divine, which lights up our brow with the glow of dawn, which lends wings to our heart and tells us that not everything in the farce is farcical, that there is something divine in our life which is true and eternal, and cannot end when the farce ends. (*Curtain*).

END OF THE PLAY

APPENDIX

I

The following is a more literal line-for-line translation of the poetry at the end of Act One:

The amorous night over lovers
spreads the nuptial canopy of its sky.
The night has fastened its bright diamonds
to the velvet of a summer sky.
The garden in shadow has no color,
and in the mystery of its darkness
the foliage is a whisper, the flowers are fragrance,
and love . . . is a sweet desire to cry.
The voice that sighs, and the voice that sings
and the voice that speaks words of love,
seem like impiety in the sacred night,
like a blasphemy in the midst of a prayer.
Soul of silence, whom I venerate,
your silence has the indescribable voice
of those who died loving in silence,
of those who stayed mute while dying of love,
of those who, while alive, because they loved us dearly,
were perhaps unable to express their love!
Is it not the voice, perchance, that I hear in the night,
and, when it says love, it says eternity?
Mother of my soul! Is it not the light of your eyes,
        the light of that star
which, like a tear of infinite love,
        trembles in the night?
Tell the woman I love today that I never loved
        anyone but you on earth,

and, since your death, I have been kissed only
by the light of that star!

* * *

Mother of my soul! I have never loved
anyone but you on earth,
and, since your death, I have been kissed only
by the light of that star!

* * *

Night, poetry, lover's madness! . . .
All must serve our turn on this occasion!
Triumph is assured! Be brave and march forward!
Who will be able to conquer us if love is ours?

II

The following is a literal translation of the clauses altered by the Doctor in his documents (page 101):

By adding a comma (and tacitly adding the accent mark to *sí*), the Doctor changes "And with the result that if he didn't declare" to "And due to the positive result, he didn't declare."

By deleting a comma, the Doctor changes "And due to the negative result, he must be condemned" to "And with the result that he shouldn't be condemned."

A CATALOG OF SELECTED DOVER BOOKS IN ALL FIELDS OF INTEREST

THE CLARINET AND CLARINET PLAYING, David Pino. Lively, comprehensive work features suggestions about technique, musicianship, and musical interpretation, as well as guidelines for teaching, making your own reeds, and preparing for public performance. Includes an intriguing look at clarinet history. "A godsend," *The Clarinet*, Journal of the International Clarinet Society. Appendixes. 7 illus. 320pp. 5⅜ x 8½. 40270-3

HOLLYWOOD GLAMOR PORTRAITS, John Kobal (ed.). 145 photos from 1926-49. Harlow, Gable, Bogart, Bacall; 94 stars in all. Full background on photographers, technical aspects. 160pp. 8⅜ x 11¼. 23352-9

THE ANNOTATED CASEY AT THE BAT: A Collection of Ballads about the Mighty Casey/Third, Revised Edition, Martin Gardner (ed.). Amusing sequels and parodies of one of America's best-loved poems: Casey's Revenge, Why Casey Whiffed, Casey's Sister at the Bat, others. 256pp. 5⅜ x 8½. 28598-7

THE RAVEN AND OTHER FAVORITE POEMS, Edgar Allan Poe. Over 40 of the author's most memorable poems: "The Bells," "Ulalume," "Israfel," "To Helen," "The Conqueror Worm," "Eldorado," "Annabel Lee," many more. Alphabetic lists of titles and first lines. 64pp. 5$^{3}/_{16}$ x 8¼. 26685-0

PERSONAL MEMOIRS OF U. S. GRANT, Ulysses Simpson Grant. Intelligent, deeply moving firsthand account of Civil War campaigns, considered by many the finest military memoirs ever written. Includes letters, historic photographs, maps and more. 528pp. 6⅛ x 9¼. 28587-1

ANCIENT EGYPTIAN MATERIALS AND INDUSTRIES, A. Lucas and J. Harris. Fascinating, comprehensive, thoroughly documented text describes this ancient civilization's vast resources and the processes that incorporated them in daily life, including the use of animal products, building materials, cosmetics, perfumes and incense, fibers, glazed ware, glass and its manufacture, materials used in the mummification process, and much more. 544pp. 6⅛ x 9¼. (Available in U.S. only.) 40446-3

RUSSIAN STORIES/RUSSKIE RASSKAZY: A Dual-Language Book, edited by Gleb Struve. Twelve tales by such masters as Chekhov, Tolstoy, Dostoevsky, Pushkin, others. Excellent word-for-word English translations on facing pages, plus teaching and study aids, Russian/English vocabulary, biographical/critical introductions, more. 416pp. 5⅜ x 8½. 26244-8

PHILADELPHIA THEN AND NOW: 60 Sites Photographed in the Past and Present, Kenneth Finkel and Susan Oyama. Rare photographs of City Hall, Logan Square, Independence Hall, Betsy Ross House, other landmarks juxtaposed with contemporary views. Captures changing face of historic city. Introduction. Captions. 128pp. 8¼ x 11. 25790-8

AIA ARCHITECTURAL GUIDE TO NASSAU AND SUFFOLK COUNTIES, LONG ISLAND, The American Institute of Architects, Long Island Chapter, and the Society for the Preservation of Long Island Antiquities. Comprehensive, well-researched and generously illustrated volume brings to life over three centuries of Long Island's great architectural heritage. More than 240 photographs with authoritative, extensively detailed captions. 176pp. 8¼ x 11. 26946-9

NORTH AMERICAN INDIAN LIFE: Customs and Traditions of 23 Tribes, Elsie Clews Parsons (ed.). 27 fictionalized essays by noted anthropologists examine religion, customs, government, additional facets of life among the Winnebago, Crow, Zuni, Eskimo, other tribes. 480pp. 6⅛ x 9¼. 27377-6

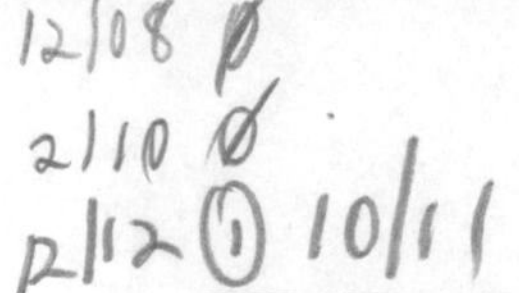

THE WIT AND HUMOR OF OSCAR WILDE, Alvin Redman (ed.). More than 1,000 ripostes, paradoxes, wisecracks: Work is the curse of the drinking classes; I can resist everything except temptation; etc. 258pp. 5⅜ x 8½. 20602-5

SHAKESPEARE LEXICON AND QUOTATION DICTIONARY, Alexander Schmidt. Full definitions, locations, shades of meaning in every word in plays and poems. More than 50,000 exact quotations. 1,485pp. 6½ x 9¼. 2-vol. set.
Vol. 1: 22726-X
Vol. 2: 22727-8

SELECTED POEMS, Emily Dickinson. Over 100 best-known, best-loved poems by one of America's foremost poets, reprinted from authoritative early editions. No comparable edition at this price. Index of first lines. 64pp. 5³⁄₁₆ x 8¼. 26466-1

THE INSIDIOUS DR. FU-MANCHU, Sax Rohmer. The first of the popular mystery series introduces a pair of English detectives to their archnemesis, the diabolical Dr. Fu-Manchu. Flavorful atmosphere, fast-paced action, and colorful characters enliven this classic of the genre. 208pp. 5³⁄₁₆ x 8¼. 29898-1

THE MALLEUS MALEFICARUM OF KRAMER AND SPRENGER, translated by Montague Summers. Full text of most important witchhunter's "bible," used by both Catholics and Protestants. 278pp. 6⅝ x 10. 22802-9

SPANISH STORIES/CUENTOS ESPAÑOLES: A Dual-Language Book, Angel Flores (ed.). Unique format offers 13 great stories in Spanish by Cervantes, Borges, others. Faithful English translations on facing pages. 352pp. 5⅜ x 8½. 25399-6

GARDEN CITY, LONG ISLAND, IN EARLY PHOTOGRAPHS, 1869–1919, Mildred H. Smith. Handsome treasury of 118 vintage pictures, accompanied by carefully researched captions, document the Garden City Hotel fire (1899), the Vanderbilt Cup Race (1908), the first airmail flight departing from the Nassau Boulevard Aerodrome (1911), and much more. 96pp. 8⅞ x 11¾. 40669-5

OLD QUEENS, N.Y., IN EARLY PHOTOGRAPHS, Vincent F. Seyfried and William Asadorian. Over 160 rare photographs of Maspeth, Jamaica, Jackson Heights, and other areas. Vintage views of DeWitt Clinton mansion, 1939 World's Fair and more. Captions. 192pp. 8⅞ x 11. 26358-4

CAPTURED BY THE INDIANS: 15 Firsthand Accounts, 1750-1870, Frederick Drimmer. Astounding true historical accounts of grisly torture, bloody conflicts, relentless pursuits, miraculous escapes and more, by people who lived to tell the tale. 384pp. 5⅜ x 8½. 24901-8

THE WORLD'S GREAT SPEECHES (Fourth Enlarged Edition), Lewis Copeland, Lawrence W. Lamm, and Stephen J. McKenna. Nearly 300 speeches provide public speakers with a wealth of updated quotes and inspiration–from Pericles' funeral oration and William Jennings Bryan's "Cross of Gold Speech" to Malcolm X's powerful words on the Black Revolution and Earl of Spenser's tribute to his sister, Diana, Princess of Wales. 944pp. 5⅜ x 8⅜. 40903-1

THE BOOK OF THE SWORD, Sir Richard F. Burton. Great Victorian scholar/adventurer's eloquent, erudite history of the "queen of weapons"–from prehistory to early Roman Empire. Evolution and development of early swords, variations (sabre, broadsword, cutlass, scimitar, etc.), much more. 336pp. 6⅛ x 9¼. 25434-8

CATALOG OF DOVER BOOKS

THE STORY OF THE TITANIC AS TOLD BY ITS SURVIVORS, Jack Winocour (ed.). What it was really like. Panic, despair, shocking inefficiency, and a little heroism. More thrilling than any fictional account. 26 illustrations. 320pp. 5⅜ x 8½. 20610-6

FAIRY AND FOLK TALES OF THE IRISH PEASANTRY, William Butler Yeats (ed.). Treasury of 64 tales from the twilight world of Celtic myth and legend: "The Soul Cages," "The Kildare Pooka," "King O'Toole and his Goose," many more. Introduction and Notes by W. B. Yeats. 352pp. 5⅜ x 8½. 26941-8

BUDDHIST MAHAYANA TEXTS, E. B. Cowell and others (eds.). Superb, accurate translations of basic documents in Mahayana Buddhism, highly important in history of religions. The Buddha-karita of Asvaghosha, Larger Sukhavativyuha, more. 448pp. 5⅜ x 8½. 25552-2

ONE TWO THREE . . . INFINITY: Facts and Speculations of Science, George Gamow. Great physicist's fascinating, readable overview of contemporary science: number theory, relativity, fourth dimension, entropy, genes, atomic structure, much more. 128 illustrations. Index. 352pp. 5⅜ x 8½. 25664-2

EXPERIMENTATION AND MEASUREMENT, W. J. Youden. Introductory manual explains laws of measurement in simple terms and offers tips for achieving accuracy and minimizing errors. Mathematics of measurement, use of instruments, experimenting with machines. 1994 edition. Foreword. Preface. Introduction. Epilogue. Selected Readings. Glossary. Index. Tables and figures. 128pp. 5⅜ x 8½. 40451-X

DALÍ ON MODERN ART: The Cuckolds of Antiquated Modern Art, Salvador Dalí. Influential painter skewers modern art and its practitioners. Outrageous evaluations of Picasso, Cézanne, Turner, more. 15 renderings of paintings discussed. 44 calligraphic decorations by Dalí. 96pp. 5⅜ x 8½. (Available in U.S. only.) 29220-7

ANTIQUE PLAYING CARDS: A Pictorial History, Henry René D'Allemagne. Over 900 elaborate, decorative images from rare playing cards (14th–20th centuries): Bacchus, death, dancing dogs, hunting scenes, royal coats of arms, players cheating, much more. 96pp. 9¼ x 12¼. 29265-7

MAKING FURNITURE MASTERPIECES: 30 Projects with Measured Drawings, Franklin H. Gottshall. Step-by-step instructions, illustrations for constructing handsome, useful pieces, among them a Sheraton desk, Chippendale chair, Spanish desk, Queen Anne table and a William and Mary dressing mirror. 224pp. 8⅛ x 11¼. 29338-6

THE FOSSIL BOOK: A Record of Prehistoric Life, Patricia V. Rich et al. Profusely illustrated definitive guide covers everything from single-celled organisms and dinosaurs to birds and mammals and the interplay between climate and man. Over 1,500 illustrations. 760pp. 7½ x 10⅛. 29371-8

12/08 Ø
12/10 Ø
12/12 ① 10/11
4/15 ③ 4/14
5/19 ④ 10/15